Praise for *Agile for Everybody*

Agile for Everybody puts culture, collaboration, and customer centricity into the focus of facilitating organizational change. Matt LeMay explains why organizations and leaders are changing their mindsets and working styles in order to have a deeper understanding of their customers and how to design and iterate quickly to create better products and work environments. *Agile for Everybody* shows how this practice is accessible to everyone who wants to improve company culture, embrace an iterative design process, and be able to react to fast-changing customer needs.

—*Jessica Covi, Creative Director, BMW Group*

If you're intrigued by Agile but wondering if it's really possible for it to work in your unique context, *Agile for Everybody* has you covered. It's a clear, concise, clever guide to evolving the Agile mindset so it seamlessly applies to knowledge work of all kinds. With this book, Matt is helping put better, faster, more innovative work within reach for everybody.

—*Andrea Fryrear, President and Lead Trainer, AgileSherpas*

As the rate of change of, literally, everything continues to accelerate, it is paramount that our understanding of how to actually "be" Agile versus "do" Agile, scales accordingly. *Agile for Everybody* takes the refreshing, and much needed, perspective of Agile as something more than tools and practices.

—*Andrew Burrows, Agile Marketing Lead, IBM*

Agile for Everybody is refreshing precisely because it exemplifies the spirit of generosity that defines Agile's origin story. There's no prescriptive finger-wagging, just a simple, honest sharing of experiences. Matt LeMay's great gift to the reader is attraction through candid storytelling. I put the book down with a few specific ideas to try, but with also a sense of possibility. In the end, that's the best feeling I can hope for when I finish a book.

—*Baron Schwartz, Founder and CTO, VividCortex*

Agile for Everybody is a masterpiece in applied learning. With this book, Matt has distilled years of Silicon Valley jargon into easy-to-learn language and an easy-to-adopt playbook for nearly every audience. This book is the perfect primer for anybody who wants to transform their organizational thinking into a proactive, problem-solving mindset through an iterative, customer-centric lens. I'm recommending this to our executive leadership team as soon as it's released.

—*Zach Harris, Senior Director, Data and Strategy,*
Children's Tumor Foundation

Agile for Everybody is a refreshing guide to seeing success from the right point of view and making it work. Without jargon, Matt shares how to understand where a team is, quick tips to improve, and why it matters. If you've seen Agile "inflicted" on projects that didn't work, the examples in this book can help you understand why. Every leader can use the Agile-focused wisdom in this book. Contained within are actionable tips for everybody: CIOs, mayors, teams large and small, police commanders, and you. The lessons fit multinational corporations, government agencies, startups, non profits, and small businesses. Reading *Agile for Everybody* will help you inspire people to do their best work with the values of Agile.

—*Andrew Nebus, Former CIO and Command Staff,*
Baltimore City Police Department

Matt's book is a perfect primer on the theory and practice of Agile. For the executive, it's a terrific guide about why you should care (happier customers, more engaged employees). For the manager, it's a great set of practical tools and advice about how Agile works and how and where it can successfully be applied (achieving quick wins, measuring success, course correcting).

—*Thomas Stubbs, Vice President, Engineering and Innovation,*
Coca-Cola Freestyle

The language and spirit of Agile is everywhere in business today. But what does it really mean and how can we act on the insights that turned a way of writing software into a way of getting almost anything done? Matt LeMay makes it clear what Agile is (and what it isn't) and reminds us what's truly valuable about the movement. *Agile for Everybody* lives up to its name.

—*Andrew Blau, Managing Director, Strategic Risk, Deloitte*

Successfully implementing Agile is about more than just changing the way you operate and execute; it is about changing your organization's entire culture. It is that culture that ultimately creates successes, failures, and all the exciting moments in between. *Agile for Everybody* is a must-read for understanding how you can bring the values and principles of Agile to your organization and to your individual work. This book makes a compelling case that Agile learning is ongoing and left me feeling particularly excited to continue evolving the practices used throughout my teams.

—*Jarrod Dicker, CEO, po.et*

Far from yet another step-by-step Agile coaching tome, *Agile for Everybody* forces us to recognize that agility does not come in a pre-sliced, neatly packaged kit. Matt LeMay illustrates the creative challenge presented when integrating Agile values with existing, complex systems. He then invites us to join him on a journey beyond the standard Agilist jargon and into the real work of cultural change.

—*Courtney Hemphill, Partner and Technical Lead, Carbon Five*

Agile practices have exploded in popularity in recent years, yet so often they are implemented in an unhelpful way, focused on velocity over impact, as if running faster without removing the blindfold were ever a good idea. As LeMay points out, speed matters, but only speed in the eyes of the customer, not the eyes of the development team. This book brings us back to the values of the Agile movement and gives us concrete and immediate recommendations for orienting our teams towards them. I highly recommend it for anyone looking to solve the right problems well.

—*Jason Stanley, Design Research Lead, Element AI*

There are many books about Agile, but none has delved into the nuances of implementing it successfully within an organization—until now. With *Agile for Everybody*, Matt has synthesized what is working today for software development teams and put together a practical guide with great shortcuts for readers.

—*Alfredo Fuentes, CTO, La Victoria Labs*

Matt LeMay demands the frequent, pointed questioning of our organizational practices that is too-often absent from today's companies. *Agile for Everybody* is, indeed, for everybody...that is, for anyone who wants to do better and be better, both in the workplace and in life.

—*David Kidder, Cofounder and CEO, Bionic*

Agile for Everybody

Creating Fast, Flexible, and Customer-First Organizations

Matt LeMay

Beijing · Boston · Farnham · Sebastopol · Tokyo

Agile for Everybody

by Matt LeMay

Copyright © 2019 Matt LeMay LLC. All rights reserved.

Published by O'Reilly Media, Inc., 1005 Gravenstein Highway North, Sebastopol, CA 95472.

O'Reilly books may be purchased for educational, business, or sales promotional use. Online editions are also available for most titles (*http://oreilly.com/safari*). For more information, contact our corporate/institutional sales department: 800-998-9938 or *corporate@oreilly.com*.

Acquitions Editor: Laurel Ruma	**Indexer:** Ellen Troutman-Zaig
Development Editor: Angela Rufino	**Interior Designer:** Monica Kamsvaag
Production Editor: Nan Barber	**Cover Designer:** Ellie Volkhausen
Copyeditor: Octal Publishing, LLC	**Illustrators:** Rebecca Demarest and Amy Martin
Proofreader: Rachel Monaghan	

The cover image, the opening images for Chapters 3 through 6, and the Organizational Gravity figures were illustrated by Amy Martin.

October 2018:   First Edition

Revision History for the First Edition

2018-10-15:   First Release

See *http://oreilly.com/catalog/errata.csp?isbn=9781492033516* for release details.

978-1-492-03351-6

[LSI]

Contents

Introduction

My Introduction to Agile: "Twice the Work in Half the Time"

We are going to be implementing some new Agile processes that will allow our product teams to get twice as much work done in half the time.

This was the first thing I heard about Agile, and I had no reason to doubt it. I was working as a product manager at a medium-sized company, and our executive team had called a company-wide meeting to share its plans for the coming year. I was not sure whether "Agile" was a *thing* with a capital A or just a general descriptor of the way we would be working moving forward, but in either case, it sounded pretty good to me. My team *had* been fairly slow to get new products out the door, in large part because changes in leadership had left us without a clear vision against which to execute. Maybe this "Agile" thing would help us solve for that? Upon returning to my desk, I quickly did a search for "Agile process," and was greeted with the following paragraph via Wikipedia:

Agile software development is a group of software development methodologies based on iterative and incremental development, where requirements and solutions evolve through collaboration between self-organizing, cross-functional teams. It promotes adaptive planning, evolutionary development and delivery, a time-boxed iterative approach, and encourages rapid and flexible response to change. It is a conceptual framework that promotes foreseen interactions throughout the development cycle. The Agile Manifesto introduced the term in 2001.

Reading this explanation left me with a creeping sense that I was far out of my depth. All of the concepts in this dense paragraph—"self-organizing," "evolutionary development," "rapid and flexible response to change"—sounded like they were almost certainly *good* things. But it was entirely unclear to me what I was supposed to *do* about any of this. What exactly is a "time-boxed iterative approach?" And how was any of this going to result in us doing twice the work in half the time?

Feeling uncertain about what was expected of me, I sought out the help and advice of some more experienced developers and designers on my team. They explained to me that Agile was a term used to describe a set of approaches that were broadly similar in spirit but different in their specific methods. The most popular of these approaches was something called *Scrum*. My colleagues recommended a few books and articles, and I set out to learn what this Scrum thing was all about and how it could help my team be faster and more efficient.

After a weekend spent reading ebooks and blog posts, I was able to glean a few tactical steps that seemed essential to implementing Scrum. First, we were to break down our work into two-week periods called *sprints*. At the end of each sprint, we were to have something actually *finished* and ready to release to our users. And during each day of the sprint, we were to have a *daily standup* or *daily scrum* meeting. During this meeting, each member of the team was to share what they've completed, what they've been working on, and what might be blocking their progress.

I reported back to my colleagues that I had read the books and articles they had recommended, and that I was ready to make some exciting changes to the way we work. The idea of actually getting something finished every two weeks seemed like a surefire boost to both productivity and morale, and having some face-to-face time every morning seemed like it could only improve our team's communication. My more experienced colleagues exchanged a kind, but knowing look. "OK," they said, "let's give it a try."

It did not take long for me to understand why my naïve enthusiasm was not necessarily shared. No sooner had we started implementing these new Agile processes than they were swiftly undermined by the very executives who had sold us on "Agile" in the first place. We began planning out work in two-week sprints, but these sprints were consistently derailed by new top-down demands and priorities. In one particular case, an executive emailed a member of my team asking that she work on something different for the duration of the sprint—and, oh, by the way, don't tell the rest of the team about this. All the dysfunction and discord that had impeded our work previously was still there. We were no faster, and we were no more efficient.

But still, something was undeniably different. In their own sneaky little ways, each of the changes we made helped us see something about our organization that had been invisible to us before. Prioritizing and committing to deliverables in two-week cycles made it clear just how often the high-level vision for the product was being pulled in conflicting directions. Checking in with one another every morning made it clear just how disconnected individual members of my team had become from our shared mission and goals. It was as though the poltergeists of organizational dysfunction that haunted us had suddenly taken a material form and were showing up, ectoplasmic coffee in hand, to our team meetings.

With these dysfunctions brought to light, my team and I were able to take some difficult but necessary steps toward actually addressing them. Disagreements between team members that would have previously affected the quality of our product were exposed in our daily meetings and then resolved in smaller follow-up conversations. I felt emboldened to push back on last-minute executive changes by pointing out that we could not get anything out the door half as fast, let alone twice as fast, if we couldn't even go two weeks without dramatically changing course. Power that had once been wielded through subterfuge and sabotage now ran up against a clear and agreed-upon set of operating procedures. In short, the silver bullet brought in by executives turned out to be more of a Trojan horse.

The Alchemy of Agile: Uniting Principles and Practices

After my initial experience with Agile, I felt like I had made a great discovery: Agile was not just about processes and tools, it was about people and culture! Though the tactical changes we made had not gone according to plan, they had brought us together as a team and helped us to understand the challenges we were facing an organization. Inspired by this realization, I began to dig a little bit deeper into the history of the Agile movement—a history we explore at greater length in Chapter 1. It did not take me long to realize that my great discovery was not much of a discovery at all. People and culture, it turned out, had been at the heart of the Agile movement all along.

This knowledge changed my approach to Agile dramatically. The human values and principles of the Agile movement provided a bright and steady North Star that my team and I could follow, even when doing a particular practice "by the book" didn't seem to be working for us. This proved particularly valuable because, as it turns out, there are a lot of different books that will tell you a lot of different things. Rather than feeling paralyzed by having to decide which of many seemingly contradictory approaches to Agile was "right," I was free to ask, "What can I pull from each of these approaches that will help the particular team I'm working with put Agile principles and values into practice?"

Indeed, the truly powerful thing about Agile is not that it provides a concrete and actionable set of practices or that it is guided by an inspiring set of principles, but rather that it necessarily involves both. Agile demands that we keep our ideals and our actions closely aligned with each other, which in turn compels us to ask some very tricky questions about why we do the things that we do as individuals, teams, and organizations.

For those who see Agile as a one-size-fits-all ticket to easy operational gains, this often comes as a nasty surprise. Even when we approach Agile in the hopes of doing more work in less time, we often find ourselves challenged to bring *more* of ourselves to the table—more energy, more openness, more willingness to reflect honestly around difficult questions. Agile, as its name suggests, asks us to be willing to challenge our assumptions and change our minds, which is no easy task.

In the decade or so since my introduction to Agile, I have seen similar stories unfold across dozens of very different organizations. I have worked with product and engineering teams at financial services organizations that adopt Agile practices in the hopes that they can better keep pace with a fast-changing world, only for those teams to realize that the inertia which they initially blamed on their leaders and their industry was largely a result of their *own* fear of change. I have worked with marketing teams at Fortune 500 consumer packaged goods companies that adopt Agile practices in the hopes of working more like cutting-edge technology companies, only for those teams to realize that they are completely unaware of the forward-thinking work being done by the R&D departments at their *own* companies. My experiences with Agile have made me a true believer, not in the sense that I believe Agile is a single solution to all the problems facing modern organizations, but rather in the sense that I believe Agile can help teams and organizations better understand and address the specific set of problems they are facing.

Why Agile for Everybody?

In a 2011 *Wall Street Journal* op-ed, venture capitalist Marc Andreessen famously declared that "software is eating the world." It is not terribly surprising, then, that the Agile principles and practices utilized by so many modern software development teams are taking a bigger and broader bite. A quick search for "Agile marketing" or "Agile sales" or "Agile leadership" yields a plethora of articles, books, and blog posts that describe how the principles and practices of Agile can be applied to a broad set of business functions. In part because of its association with the high-tech world of software development, "Agile" has become a popular prefix for all kinds of cutting-edge business activities, just as "digital" was in the late 1990s and early 2000s.

In theory, the idea of extending the core ideas of Agile beyond software development seems like a logical next step. As we discuss in Chapter 1, the founders of the Agile movement were keenly aware that the values and principles they espouse are relevant and applicable throughout modern organizations, well beyond product and engineering teams. At their best, these values and principles provide a shared language that can break down functional silos and unite organizations in collaborative, customer-centric work.

In practice, however, there is a substantial risk that the growth of Agile into other areas of business will actually reinforce organizational silos rather than break them down. Every function within a business has its own specific jargon, its own specific tools, and its own specific frameworks and methodologies. If we treat, say, "Agile software development," "Agile sales," and "Agile marketing" as distinct and function-specific collections of tactics and methods, we are missing out on a critical opportunity to work together toward meeting the needs of our customers. In other words, we run the risk of "Agile for X" and "Agile for Y" highlighting and exacerbating the differences between X and Y rather than uniting different functions around the common values of the Agile movement.

Thus, *Agile for Everybody*. My goal with this book was to answer two questions: how can we frame the underlying principles of Agile in a way that is equally accessible and instructive for individuals across roles and functions, and what can we actually *do* in our day-to-day work to put these principles into practice?

In my work as a consultant and trainer, I have found these questions to be just as impactful for product and engineering teams at small startups as they are for marketing and insights teams at Fortune 500 enterprises. The specific approaches used by these teams to put Agile values and principles into practices are, necessarily, quite different. But starting with these values and principles creates a shared language and a shared vision that can transcend functions, titles, and even organizations. It casts Agile as a broad and inclusive movement in which all of our contributions and perspectives have value. And it gives us precious few excuses for abandoning our efforts if and when we find that doing Agile "by the book" isn't moving us in the direction we had hoped.

To that end, the word *Agile* is used throughout this book to refer to the overall set of practices, principles, and values that are widely associated with the Agile movement. Many of the practices described in this book originate from specific Agile software development methodologies, but have been generalized to reflect the broader colloquial use of the term. In the interest of extending the Agile movement beyond product and engineering teams, I have found it much more actionable to take a "that's also" approach (as in, "That's also something we can do to put Agile values into practice!") than a "that's actually" approach (as in, "That's actually part of *this* Agile methodology, not *that* Agile methodology"). Our goal, after all, is to change the way we work for the better, which means prioritizing practical action over theoretical debate.

Who This Book Is For

This book is for anybody who believes that customer centricity, collaboration, and openness to change should be at the heart of modern organizations.

In the words of one of its cofounders (*http://bit.ly/2DX9x8v*), the Agile movement was founded upon "a set of values based on trust and respect for each other and promoting organizational models based on people, collaboration, and building the types of organizational communities in which we would want to work." Those values, and the practices that enact them, can offer a much-needed path forward for organizations struggling with hierarchies, silos, and rote and restrictive processes.

This book is designed to provide a holistic, actionable, and accessible overview of the "why," "how," and "what" of Agile. It outlines the principles, practices, and success signals that individuals can use to bring the best of Agile to their organization across roles, teams, and functions. This is the book I have wanted to hand to executives when they tell me, "I've heard this Agile thing can make us a faster and more innovative organization," and the book I have wanted to hand to people in marketing, sales, and consulting roles when they say, "We don't make software, so I'm not sure how Agile could work for us."

For organizational leaders in particular, I hope this book can convey a sense of the candor, reflection, and hard work that goes into truly embracing the principles of Agile. Experienced Agile practitioner Lane Goldstone, one of the many inspiring people I interviewed for this book, stated it perfectly: "If this book results in even one executive being more thoughtful and humane in their deployment of Agile, I think it will be a success."

How I Wrote This Book

This book began with conversations—a *lot* of conversations—between myself and Agile practitioners from dozens of different companies, industries, and roles. Some work in manufacturing, some work in the nonprofit sector, some work in marketing, and some work in sales. Some are VPs and C-suite executives at multinational corporations; some are independent practitioners and consultants. Some are formally trained Scrum masters and Agile coaches, while some have never really thought about the work they do as particularly "Agile." All were exceptionally generous with sharing their real-world experiences—good, bad, or ugly—and speaking candidly to both the power and the limitations of the approaches they've taken.

Many of the people I spoke with described how their most successful experiences with Agile have involved drawing upon ideas and practices from multiple toolsets, frameworks, and methodologies, some of which are not formally considered part of Agile at all. And none of the people I spoke with claimed to have figured out the single best or most correct approach to Agile. People working in real-world organizations generally don't have the luxury of dogmatic certainty—they have products to build, campaigns to launch, and people to get along with. It follows, then, that the stories from Agile practitioners that are peppered throughout this book are not intended as a prescriptive set of the "best" ways for any team or organization to approach Agile principles and practices. Instead, they provide some real-world examples of how people across functions and industries have used Agile principles and practices to meet the needs of their specific teams, organizations, and customers. This book, as with any book, can't do the work for you. But it can help you understand the work that *you* need to do.

How This Book Is Organized

This book is designed to provide you with the raw materials you need to approach Agile principles and practices in a meaningful, sustainable, and future-proof way. Doing so requires identifying and articulating *why* you are turning toward Agile in the first place, *how* you plan to put Agile principles into practice, and *what* real-world outcomes you are achieving for your colleagues and your customers. This approach creates a sustainable, self-reinforcing loop, as shown in Figure I-1.

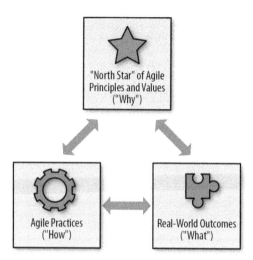

Figure I-1. Keeping principles, practices, and real-world outcomes synchronized.

First and foremost, any meaningful implementation of Agile must begin with a clear sense of *why* a given organization or team is looking to change the way it works in the first place. To find the unique North Star of Agile principles and values that represent your "Why," you can take two steps that we discuss in more detail in Chapter 2: identifying the goals of your particular organization or team, and then using those goals to articulate the underlying principles of Agile in a way that will be recognizable, meaningful, and actionable for your specific context.

After you've found your "Why," you can begin identifying the particular Agile practices that you will use to change *how* your team or organization works. As we discuss in Chapter 6, actually implementing these practices often involves starting small and generating a "pull" across teams and functions rather than trying to "push" a new way of working to everybody all at the same time.

Finally, you must pay close and unflinching attention to the real-world outcomes that your chosen Agile practices are creating for your colleagues and customers. Note that I have explicitly defined "What" not as "What are the Agile practices we will implement," but rather as "What is *actually happening* as we implement these practices and follow our guiding principles?" This is to ensure that we do not confuse the adoption of Agile practices with the outcomes that we hope they will enable us to achieve for our colleagues and our customers.

These three pieces form a feedback loop that we can use to sustain and adapt our Agile journey as our markets, our customers, and our own organizational structures change. If we feel that we are not living up to our North Star of Agile values and principles ("Why"), we can reevaluate the practices we have chosen to activate them ("How"). If we feel that these practices are not resulting in a better working experience for our colleagues and higher-quality outcomes for our customers ("What"), we can reevaluate our North Star ("Why") to see whether it still reflects our best understanding of our organization, our market, and our customers.

AGILE GUIDING PRINCIPLES ("WHY")

The first step of any successful Agile journey is understanding *why* you want to change the way you work in the first place. In Chapter 2, we take a closer look at the steps you can take to understand your particular goals—and how you can use those goals to articulate the Agile values and principles that will guide your organization or team. For the purposes of this book, the difference between "values" and "principles" is purely semantic; a statement of values ("we value X over Y"), a statement of principles ("we believe X, Y, and Z"), or a combination of both can provide meaningful and substantive guidance.

Chapters 3 through 6 are organized around three guiding principles of Agile for everybody:

- Agile means that we start with our customers
- Agile means that we collaborate early and often
- Agile means that we plan for uncertainty

These three guiding principles represent my attempt to synthesize and distill the underlying ideas from the Agile movement that I have found to be most impactful across functions, industries, and organizations. This approach is inspired by Agile movement cofounder Alistair Cockburn, who distilled the principles and practices of Agile into his own set of straightforward, jargon-free prompts called "The Heart of Agile (*http://heartofagile.com/*)": "Collaborate, Deliver, Reflect, Improve."

Distilling Agile to a set of simple prompts allows teams from any function or industry to accommodate the realities of their own work and still make room for positive change. For example, a marketing team could ask, "Are we collaborating early and often?" to identify new opportunities for working more closely with their counterparts in product. A sales team could ask, "Are we planning for uncertainty?" to think through different scenarios for how to adjust course if they appear to be missing their targets. These prompts themselves do not provide absolute prescriptive solutions, but they can help lead us to solutions that are both impactful and achievable.

AGILE PRACTICE QUICK WINS AND DEEP DIVES ("HOW")

Within Chapters 3 through 6, I share a few examples of steps that teams and individuals in different roles (such as sales, marketing, and executives) could take to put a given Agile principle into practice. These are meant to be lightweight, approachable activities that introduce Agile practices to your team without demanding too much commitment or buy-in. I've often found it helpful to frame these activities as little experiments that you can easily roll back if they are deemed unsuccessful; that is, "Let's try this out for a while, and see what happens! Worse comes to worst, we can always go back to doing things the way we did before."

In each of these four chapters, I also share a deep dive into a common Agile practice that provides teams and organizations with a tangible way to make each guiding principle a part of their day-to-day work. The goal of these deep dives is to help you understand how you can use each practice to actualize and reinforce Agile principles—and to help you identify situations in which simply implementing these practices might *not* be helping you to actualize and reinforce those principles.

There are, of course, many more than four practices contained within formalized Agile methodologies and countless others beyond those methodologies. If you are interested in learning more about these practices, I strongly recommend checking out the subway map of Agile methodologies and practices (*http://bit.ly/2NdLzF7*) provided by the Agile Alliance.

SUCCESS SIGNALS AND WARNING SIGNS ("WHAT")

Agile practices always play out differently in the real world from how they do on paper, and it is critical that you remain well attuned to what is actually happening to your organization and your customers as you implement these practices. Although every organization's Agile journey is different, there are a few common success signals and warning signs that are worth looking out for. These are captured in Chapter 3 through Chapter 6 under the headings "You might be on the right track if…" and "You might be going astray if…" For each success signal, you will find a few tips and pointers for keeping the momentum going. For each warning sign, you will find a few tips and pointers for getting back on track.

YOUR AGILE PLAYBOOK

Finally, in Chapter 7, you have the opportunity to combine the principles and practices you've read about into an "Agile playbook" for your own team. This is a similar exercise to one you might go through with an Agile coach, and I strongly recommend that everybody who reads this book completes it. In going through these steps, you might realize that there are some difficult questions your team needs to talk through together, or that a few small changes to the way you work could have an outsized impact.

Acknowledgments

Nodding along to the general principles of the Agile movement is quite easy, but actually following them is incredibly difficult. Throughout the process of writing this book, I found myself exhibiting some of the very behaviors for which I have admonished "Agile" teams and organizations. I balked at the idea of sharing works in progress for fear that they would not be suitably impressive. I resisted new information that complicated my preexisting beliefs and ideas. And I became frustrated when this new information called for me to rework things I had already written, even when I knew the book would be stronger for it.

All of which is to say, the process of writing this book constituted its own kind of Agile journey for me personally. I am deeply and profoundly grateful to everybody who took the time to provide their input and feedback, both on and off the record. The stories and perspectives included in this book have proven inspiring and instructive, both professionally and personally, and it is a true honor to share them here.

I am also deeply and profoundly grateful to my wife, Joan, who can see things I cannot see and is always brave and generous enough to voice them. And to my mom, Carol, a skilled communicator by nature and by trade, who helped distill and clarify many of the concepts in this book. Many of those concepts emerged directly from the work I have done with my Sudden Compass business partners, Tricia Wang and Sunny Bates, whose support and partnership mean the world to me.

Enormous thanks to everybody at O'Reilly Media, both for shepherding this book into existence and for giving me the opportunity to road test its content via trainings and videos. Enormous thanks to Lane Goldstone, Courtney Hemphill, and the Balanced Team NY community for giving me the opportunity to test some of the ideas in this book with skilled and experienced practitioners. And enormous thanks to Amy Martin, whose illustrations perfectly capture the human dimension of Agile. You can find more of Amy's amazing work at *http://www.amymartinillustration.com/*.

This book is dedicated to everybody who has been brave enough to challenge the status quo and seek out new and better ways of working, whether or not they are called "Agile."

What Is Agile, and Why Does It Matter?

Understanding Agile as a Movement

On February 11–13, 2001, at The Lodge at Snowbird ski resort in the Wasatch mountains of Utah, seventeen people met to talk, ski, relax, and try to find common ground—and of course, to eat.

So begins the story (*http://bit.ly/2DX9x8v*) of the Agile movement as told by one of its originators, Jim Highsmith.

It is worth taking a moment to reflect on the humility—and humanity—of this statement. The Agile movement was not born out of an ambition to sell books or rack up consulting hours. It was born out of the very belief that animates its most successful implementations: when people come together, look beyond the tactical differences in their respective approaches, and seek common ground, amazing things can happen.

The 17 people who gathered at Snowbird had spent the better part of the prior decade looking for ways to bring this kind of collaboration to their day-to-day work as software developers. Some of them had begun implementing daily "stand-up" meetings to create more space for regular conversation. Some of them were encouraging their colleagues to work in pairs, maximizing the transfer of knowledge and revealing previously unseen solutions. Some of them were looking at how organizational processes themselves could become "stretch to fit" to better suit the needs of the specific individuals on a given team.

By the time the Snowbird summit took place, some of these practices had evolved into fully formed methodologies with names like Scrum, Extreme Programming, and Crystal. But those gathered at Snowbird were not interested in debating which of their methodologies was the best. Instead, they wanted to see if 17 self-described "organizational anarchists" could identify the common themes, values, and principles underlying their respective practices, frameworks, and methodologies. By all accounts, nobody thought this would be an easy task.

To the great surprise of many people in attendance, deciding on a shared set of values proved much less contentious than deciding where to hold the summit in the first place. By the end of their gathering, this group had agreed upon a word to describe the ideas that connected and united their respective approaches: *Agile*. And they had captured their shared values in a document called the *Manifesto for Agile Software Development*.

Here is the text of what has come to be known colloquially as "the Agile Manifesto," in its entirety:

> We are uncovering better ways of developing
> software by doing it and helping others do it.
> Through this work we have come to value:
>
> **Individuals and interactions** over *processes and tools*
> **Working software** over *comprehensive documentation*
> **Customer collaboration** over *contract negotiation*
> **Responding to change** over *following a plan*
>
> That is, while there is value in the items on
> the right, we value the items on the left more.

That's it. Sixty-eight words. Note that none of these words speak to specific practices, tools, or methodologies, except to say that tools are explicitly *less* valuable than *people*. According to Highsmith, this was no accident:

> At the core, I believe Agile Methodologists are really about "mushy" stuff—about delivering good products to customers by operating in an environment that does more than talk about "people as our most important asset" but actually "acts" as if people were the most important, and lose the word "asset." So in the final analysis, the meteoric rise of interest in—and sometimes tremendous criticism of—Agile Methodologies is about the mushy stuff of values and culture.

At the heart of the Agile movement, in both its substance and its history, is the belief that hard methodologies and "mushy" values cannot and should not be disentangled from each other. Methodologies must be driven by culture and values, and culture and values must be enacted through tangible practices.

It is for this very reason that I bristle a little bit whenever I hear Agile referred to as simply a "methodology." Yes, there are a number of methodologies—including the aforementioned Scrum, Extreme Programming, and Crystal, as well as those more recently developed, such as SAFe and LeSS—that provide a blueprint for how we can put Agile values into practice. But you need not look all that closely at the 68 words of the Agile Manifesto to understand why framing Agile as a *process* or a *tool* can easily miss the point.

I have also heard Agile referred to as a "mindset." While I agree that Agile requires a substantial shift in thinking, I feel like describing it as a "mindset" lets us off the hook too easily. Just *thinking* in an Agile way is not enough, and it leaves an awful lot of room for us to say, "Well, I understand this whole Agile thing, but the people I'm working with just haven't adopted this new mindset, so there's nothing we can do about it!" Table 1-1 compares these different approaches to Agile, and demonstrates how framing Agile as a movement makes it possible for us to change both our methodology and our mindset, and to keep these two dimensions synchronized as we go.

Table 1-1. Agile as a methodology, a mindset, and a movement

Agile as a methodology	Agile as a mindset	Agile as a movement
Practices matter more than mindset.	Mindset matters more than practices.	Mindset and practices are inexorably connected.
The practices and methods of Agile were already determined by others.	The principles and values of Agile were already determined by others.	I have an active role to play in determining how Agile principles and practices are articulated and applied in my team or organization.
Individuals within teams must collaborate and interact in prescribed and predefined ways.	Individuals within teams must independently develop an Agile "mindset."	Individuals within teams must work together toward a shared set of goals and values.

For all of these reasons, I am inclined to agree with Highsmith himself when he describes Agile as a *movement*. Embracing Agile as a movement helps us to better understand our own responsibilities around bringing its practices and principles to our own work in several ways:

Agile is a single movement that emerged from parallel innovation

Much like other important movements in work, culture, and art, Agile emerged when multiple practitioners developed independent but parallel innovations in response to changes in the world around them. The impressionist painting movement, for example, emerged as a number of painters reacted in parallel against the rigid academic rules of the time, and to the popularization of photography. Similarly, the Agile movement emerged as a number of software developers reacted in parallel against the rigid conditions of corporate work, and to the accelerating pace of technological change, as shown in Figure 1-1. Seeing Agile through the lens of parallel innovation helps us to understand how our own contributions can continue to push the movement forward.

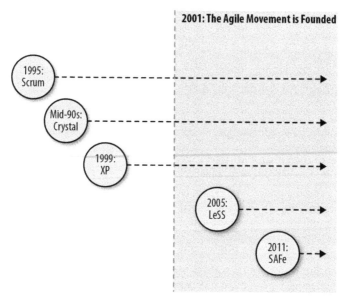

Figure 1-1. A partial timeline of Agile frameworks and methodologies by the year they are widely considered to have been formalized. Note how new frameworks and methodologies have continued to emerge and evolve after the movement's founding.

Agile demands both thought and action

When we think of Agile as a movement, it sets a high bar for both thought *and* action. Movements require a new way of thinking and a new way of working, and they demand that we keep these two things constantly synchronized with each other. If we do the work thoughtlessly, we are at best making minor operational tweaks. And if we do not support our thought with action, we are creating a deep and dangerous divide between what we say and what we do.

Agile compels us to work together toward a greater good

Framing Agile as a movement makes it clear that it is something we must do *together*. Agile asks us to be open, collaborative, and reflective. It asks us to look beyond the "correct" implementation of processes and tools, accept our uniqueness and complexity as individuals, and find ways in which we can work together toward a greater good—just as the signers of the Agile Manifesto did when they gathered in Utah.

In many ways, the story of the Agile movement contains within itself the blueprint for a successful implementation of Agile: accept the fact that different teams benefit from different tactical approaches, find common ground in shared values, and keep moving forward.

Unpacking the Appeal of Agile

The Agile Alliance, an organization formed by the 17 signers of the Agile Manifesto, defines Agile (*https://www.agilealliance.org/agile101/*) simply as "the ability to create and respond to change in order to succeed in an uncertain and turbulent environment."

It is not terribly difficult to see why this is so compelling to modern organizations. The idea that our world is faster-paced, more connected, and more customer-driven than ever before is table stakes for any contemporary discussion about organizational design and culture. Modern organizations—especially large, slow-moving enterprises—exist in constant terror of being "disrupted" by smaller and more adaptable players. The sense of urgency around becoming faster, more flexible, and more customer-centric is real. And Agile provides a material answer to the question, "How can we be more like the cutting-edge technology companies and startups that might put us out of business?"

However, the idea that Agile is some kind of magical secret that provides high-tech companies with an intrinsic competitive advantage is a gross and misleading oversimplification. Many of the folks I've worked with at large traditional companies are genuinely shocked to hear that the technology companies that they both fear and idolize are not the egalitarian hives of free-snack-fueled innovation that you read about in rosy PR statements or fawning press profiles. For better or worse, these companies often face many of the same underlying challenges that more traditional companies do: a tendency to be more management-centric than customer-centric, organizational silos that stifle collaboration, and resistance to change after a project is set in motion.

Many folks I've worked with are also surprised and disheartened to hear that "working like a small startup" in no way guarantees a successful realization of Agile values. Startup founders, especially those puffed up by millions of dollars in venture funding and our current cultural obsession with entrepreneurship, can be among the least genuinely adaptable people I've ever met. For better or worse, a high-tech organization of five people can be just as insular, noncommunicative, and set in its ways as a traditional business of 5,000 people.

Ultimately, embracing a truly Agile approach means giving up on the idea that any set of rules or practices will confer an immediate competitive advantage or high-tech halo. It's all right there in the first sentence of the Agile Manifesto: our teams and organizations are much more a product of the *people* we work with than they are a product of the *processes* we implement. At its best, Agile can remove some of the friction that comes from working against the fast-moving and unpredictable nature of the world around us, making it easier for individuals and teams to do their best work. But Agile cannot turn a bank into a search engine or an enterprise into a startup.

Escaping Business as Usual

The Agile Manifesto states unequivocally that individuals and interactions are to be valued above processes and tools. And while this statement of values is easy to agree with in theory, it presents some enormous challenges in practice. Processes and tools are generally visible, material, and relatively easy to change. But the forces shaping individuals and their interactions are often invisible, unspoken, and very difficult to change. It is very rare that somebody will come out and say, for example, "I might get fired if I tell my boss about the negative feedback I received from a customer, so I will intentionally withhold that feedback." But it is not at all uncommon for individuals working in organizations to be very selective about what information they actually provide to their managers—or seek out from customers in the first place. Their managers, meanwhile, are often left wondering, "Why didn't anybody tell me that this was a bad idea?"

Scenarios like this continue to play out day after day in organization after organization, regardless of the fancy frameworks and shiny high-tech tools those organizations adopt. Even in organizations whose leadership is committed to pursuing meaningful change, the forces keeping people tethered to "business as usual" can feel as pervasive and inescapable as gravity itself. Thus, they are often manifest in what I call the *Three Laws of Organizational Gravity*:

- Individuals in an organization will avoid customer-facing work if it is not aligned with their day-to-day responsibilities and incentives.

- Individuals in an organization will prioritize the work that they can complete most easily within the comfort of their own team or silo.

- A project in motion will stay in motion unless acted upon by the seniormost person who approved it.

The example described earlier is one manifestation of the Third Law of Organizational Gravity: if somebody's manager approved a project, that person is unlikely to call that project into question, regardless of what they hear from customers—and, ultimately, regardless of how their manager might actually react upon hearing this feedback. We are creatures of habit, and many modern organizations represent the sum total of the habits and expectations we've built up after years of navigating "business as usual."

Framing up these dynamics as a matter of organizational gravity helps us unpack the all-too-common situations in which the path of least resistance feels irreconcilably at odds with the best interest of our colleagues and our customers. It helps build empathy and understanding for organizational leaders whose attempts to manage this tension might seem hypocritical or duplicitous. And it helps us understand how our own day-to-day behaviors might be contributing to the very problems we are trying to solve. In Chapters 3 through 5 we take a closer look at each of the Three Laws of Organizational Gravity and discuss how our guiding principles of Agile can help us escape them.

Agile Versus Waterfall

The practices associated with the Agile movement are often presented as an alternative to traditional *Waterfall* approaches to product and project management. The comparison usually goes like this: in a Waterfall approach, each stage of a product or project's development is executed by a separate team with a separate, distinct skill set. A team of business or subject matter experts, for example, might be responsible for creating the initial plan for a product. They then hand it off to another team, which is responsible for designing that product. That team then hands it off to yet another team that handles building the product. It is often months, or even years, before anything is actually finished—but the thing that is finished, at least in theory, is the exact thing that was initially planned.

An Agile approach, by contrast, involves a cross-functional team releasing smaller finished outputs in shorter cycles, as shown in Figure 1-2. The term "cross-functional" usually denotes a team in which all the skills needed to see a project through from planning to execution are represented in a single team. This team works together to complete smaller outputs within finite and consistent periods of time, often called *time boxes*. The output of each time box is released to its intended audience, and the feedback gathered from that audience is used to direct and prioritize future time-boxed outputs, often called *iterations*. Thus, something of value can be delivered quickly—but as time goes on, the "completed" product or project can deviate substantially from the initial plan.

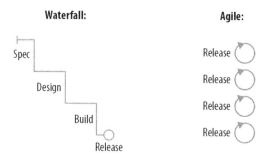

Figure 1-2. Waterfall (left) involves multiple handoffs between specialized teams, leading to a single highly planned release. Agile (right) involves a cross-functional team releasing more frequently, gathering feedback, and adjusting course as needed.

By way of example, imagine that you were building a website for a brick-and-mortar retail company. In a traditional Waterfall approach, you would create a lengthy specification, or "spec," which is a document that outlines exactly the features you want on your website, how you want those features to work, and what you want the overall look and feel of the site to be. You would then hand off that spec to a team of designers, who would provide a visual mockup of the site's specific pages and elements. After you approve those mockups, you would then hand them off to a team of developers, who would transform them into a functioning website that matches as closely as possible the original spec you wrote. In six months, you would have a fully functioning website.

Now, let's imagine that you were building that same website using an Agile approach. The team tasked with creating the site would include both designers *and* developers, and you would be working with them to prioritize smaller releases based on your needs and those of your customers. You might decide, for example, to spend your first two-week time box creating a basic landing page that provides customers with information about your store. You might then decide to spend your next two-week time box creating a simple email mailing list with weekly specials and offers. In four weeks, you might have something that is already contributing to the growth of your business, even if it is not the full-featured website you had in mind.

It is, frankly, difficult to compare Agile and Waterfall in a way that doesn't seem to give the clear advantage to Agile. In theory, meticulously prioritized and tightly scoped releases always seem more appealing than hundred-page specs, transactional handoffs, and months-long project plans.

In practice, though, it is rarely this simple. Imagine, for example, that you are working on a product in a highly regulated industry such as banking or medicine. A basic legal review might require months of time from a team of very well-compensated lawyers. If those lawyers don't have a chance to review a complete and comprehensive project plan, there is a high likelihood that your design and engineering teams will produce something that simply cannot be released, resulting in lost time and lost money. How are you supposed to be Agile in such an environment?

These challenges become even more confounding for teams that are not building a product in the traditional sense. Marketing and sales teams, for example, are often highly dependent upon yearly budgeting cycles. Agencies working on major ad campaigns must work backward from fixed deadlines and incorporate both structured and ad hoc feedback from their clients. In the real world, even our best Agile intentions rarely lead us to something that looks or feels like a bunch of neat little circles in a row. When we approach Agile as an absolute and inflexible set of operational rules, small but positive changes to the way we work can feel like trivial steps toward an end state that is perpetually out of reach. When we take a principles-first approach to Agile, small but positive changes to the way we work can create a powerful sense of momentum and possibility.

For these reasons, it is important that we look for opportunities to apply the principles of Agile to our day-to-day work even if a textbook Agile approach seems impossible. If, for example, we are organized into large and functionally siloed teams, how can we encourage more interaction across teams? How can we make each handoff between teams more collaborative and less transactional? And how can we more closely involve our customer every step of the way?

Agile, Lean, and Design Thinking

Unsurprisingly, the signers of the Agile Manifesto are not the only people who have spent the past couple of decades thinking about new ways of working. Along with Agile, several adjacent movements and approaches, including but not limited to *Lean* and *Design Thinking*, have come to prominence as organizations look for new ways to work quickly and adaptably.

The Lean movement traces its origins back to the automobile manufacturers of the early 20th century, who sought to minimize waste and overproduction. Lean manufacturing provided some of the inspiration for foundational Agile methodologies such as Scrum and was explicitly applied to the world of Agile software development in 2003 when Mary and Tom Poppendieck published *Lean Software Development: An Agile Toolkit*. In 2011, Eric Ries extended the Lean movement further beyond its manufacturing roots with the publication of *The Lean Startup* (*http://theleanstartup.com/*), a popular business title arguing that, in today's environment of great uncertainty, anything that does not contribute to learning about customers is, in Lean parlance, *waste*.

Design Thinking is, in the words of IDEO CEO Tim Brown, "a human-centered approach to innovation that draws from the designer's toolkit to integrate the needs of people, the possibilities of technology, and the requirements for business success." In practice, Design Thinking often involves conducting interviews to better understand customer needs, brainstorming several potential solutions, and rapidly prototyping these solutions to test for usability and desirability.

Extending the idea of "parallel innovation" that birthed the Agile movement, we can see how these movements are in many ways addressing the same fundamental question: *how can organizations adapt to meet the needs of customers in a fast-changing world?* Though each of these movements answers the question slightly differently, they are all driven by a similar set of values around customer centricity, collaboration, and openness to change.

As product designer and researcher Dr. Anna Harrison pointed out to me, perhaps the most meaningful difference in these approaches is not the approaches themselves, but rather how organizations measure their respective success, as shown in Figure 1-3. Broadly speaking, organizations tend to measure the success of Agile initiatives by velocity, or the speed at which they can release products to market. Organizations tend to measure the success of a Lean initiative by efficiency, or the amount of waste they can eliminate from the production process. And organizations tend to measure the success of a Design Thinking initiative by usability, or the amount of value their products can provide to customers.

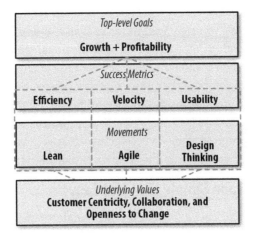

Figure 1-3. *Agile and adjacent movements mapped to the success metrics against which they are commonly measured. This can be a helpful diagnostic for understanding an organization's perceived priorities.*

Which of these three movements an organization first chooses to pursue is sometimes a sign of which of these three success metrics it perceives to be most important. Other times, it is simply a matter of which book or article an organizational leader happens to have read first. It is not uncommon for different teams within an organization to find themselves separately exploring the principles and practices of these movements at the same time. A product team, for example, might find itself in a series of Lean Startup workshops, only for its counterparts in marketing to kick off an Agile marketing initiative. Or, perhaps more commonly, an organization might be putting its engineers through Agile training and its product managers and designers through Design Thinking training, leaving both groups with a whole lot of questions about whether these approaches are duplicative, complementary, or in conflict with one another.

It is only through grappling with these questions that many organizations come to realize just how closely aligned these three movements are, and that it is ultimately up to *them* to implement principles and practices from each that best meet their specific needs and goals. As IBM Distinguished Engineer Bill Higgins told me, "After working with both Agile and Design Thinking, we got to the point of saying that the outcomes of these two approaches are highly aligned. The differences tend to be in some of the terminology—oftentimes different terms for some of the same concepts."

All of which is to say that if you're worried about choosing the wrong approach—don't be. Many of the concepts discussed in this book will overlap substantially with those you may encounter in books and articles about Lean or Design Thinking or other approaches to organizational design and leadership such as Six Sigma. When you have a clear sense of the change you want to see in your team or organization, and the values that you believe will drive that change, you will likely find something useful in *every* different approach you encounter. The challenge is not so much to select which approach is the most correct, but rather to be clear enough in your own objectives that you can find the elements of each approach that are best suited to your particular needs and goals.

Summary: Agile Made Simple (But Not Easy)

The world of Agile can seem like a dizzying tangle of methodologies, frameworks, rules, and rituals. But the expansive nature of Agile is in no way a symptom of intrinsic complexity—in fact, quite the opposite is true. The tactics of Agile can seem so complex and contradictory precisely because the underlying values of Agile are so simple, accessible, and broadly applicable. Within this set of values there is plenty of room for a wide, diverse, and differentiated set of approaches, which makes it possible for us to bring Agile to teams and organizations with a wide, diverse, and differentiated set of needs. When we approach Agile as a movement driven by values and principles, we are insisting that there is also room for *us* to figure out how best to put these values and principles into practice in a way that meets the needs of our particular teams and organizations. In doing so, we take on the responsibility of serving as active stewards of the Agile movement, not just passive followers.

2

Finding Your North Star

Escaping the Frameworks Trap

This is how we're doing things, so get out.

This was the message given to an experienced Agile coach tasked with transforming a transportation company in the United Kingdom. His crime? Asking *why*.

This company, like many companies, had picked out an Agile framework that it was convinced would deliver the speed and flexibility it desired. The framework this company chose came with new, fancy vocabulary. It came with a set of easy-to-follow rituals. It came with the promise that if these rituals were observed to the letter, this company would be able to work faster and more efficiently than ever before.

But this Agile coach, having been through this kind of thing before, was not interested in following the letter of the law without having a candid conversation about the intent of the law. "Why did we choose this particular framework?" "What are the principles we are following in our implementation?" "How will this be different from the way we are currently working?" These were the exact questions that members of this team did not want to ask, and they made this known in no uncertain terms.

Six months later, another Agile coach working with the same company returned to check on its progress. This Agile coach described the situation to me as follows:

They had become "experts" in the methodology they chose—but they were basically doing everything the same way that they had before, just with different jargon. "Instead of doing this meeting, we're going to do

THIS one." Same meeting, different name. "Instead of doing this documentation, we're going to do THAT documentation." Same documentation, different name. They had done nothing to address the fundamental challenges that they were facing as an organization, and had done nothing to create a more accessible, open, and transparent culture. Instead, it was all about playing work, having this new title, having this new lingo.

Without even realizing it, this company had fallen deep into the frameworks trap: implementing a specific set of Agile practices *without* taking the time to understand the underlying issues that it was actually trying to address, or the principles that it would follow to address them. As shown in Figure 2-1, organizations often approach new frameworks and practices in the general hopes of being faster, more flexible, and broadly *better* than they were before, only to find themselves right back where they started.

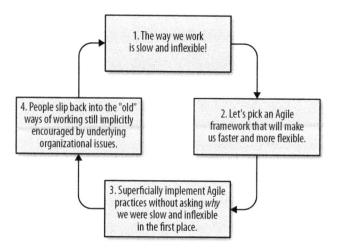

Figure 2-1. The frameworks trap—rinse and repeat!

As this story illustrates, organizations often fall into the frameworks trap not only because they believe a single framework will magically solve all their existing problems, but also because they actively resist having a conversation about what exactly their existing problems might be and how Agile might help them solve those problems.

It is for this reason, perhaps, that many organizations and teams find it safer to approach Agile as a set of operational rules rather than as a movement guided by principles and values. In a blog post titled "The Failure of Agile (*http://bit.ly/ 2Qp8iAa*)," Agile Manifesto signer Andy Hunt describes why the "joy of rules" can lead organizations to superficial and ultimately fruitless implementations of Agile practices:

> *Instead of looking up to the agile principles and the abstract ideas of the agile manifesto, folks get as far as the perceived iron rules of a set of practices, and no further.*

> *Agile methods ask practitioners to think, and frankly, that's a hard sell. It is far more comfortable to simply follow what rules are given and claim you're "doing it by the book." It's easy, it's safe from ridicule or recrimination; you won't get fired for it. While we might publicly decry the narrow confines of a set of rules, there is safety and comfort there. But of course, to be agile—or effective—isn't about comfort.*

Indeed, any rules that are followed without a clear and well-understood purpose are useless by their very nature because their intended use has never been defined. As Hunt suggests, this entirely rules-based approach allows teams and organizations to superficially adopt "correct" practices without interrogating what was "incorrect" about the way they were accustomed to working, ultimately leaving any and all underlying issues unaddressed. This is a painfully common pattern for "organizational transformations" and reorganizations of all kinds, including but by no means limited to those labeled "Agile." Here are four common signs that you might be falling into the frameworks trap:

That last framework or methodology you tried was a disaster, so you're trying a new one!

> Teams and organizations stuck in the frameworks trap often have very strong opinions about the frameworks and methodologies they've implemented in the past. "Oh yeah, we tried Scrum, and it was a *total disaster*— so now we're switching to a scaled framework." A few months later, "That scaled framework we chose just had *nothing* to do with the way we work, so we're going to try out a different one." Usually, by the third or fourth failed Agile initiative, you begin to hear things like, "I just don't understand all this hype around Agile, but we just spoke to a consultant who specializes in Lean Six Sigma, and I think that's going to be a much better fit for us." Meanwhile, business as usual continues.

"Talking Agile" is considered "being Agile"

Organizations that implement Agile superficially often become fixated on that most superficial of all things: jargon. Agile terminology is trotted out relentlessly at meetings, and anybody who furrows their brow at the idea of "daily scrum meetings" or "time-boxed iterations" is met with a dismissive eye-roll or smug smirk. Those who dare to ask "why" are accused of "not getting it." Nonetheless, business as usual continues.

Conversations about what isn't working for this organization are rebutted with tales from other organizations

"This framework completely transformed Company X" can be a persuasive argument, especially when voiced by somebody who actually worked at Company X. Not wanting to push back against something that has been proven to work (or, at least, is the subject of a glowing case study), organizations will often double down on frameworks and practices that are quite obviously not delivering positive outcomes. Faced with this disconnect, employees are left to conclude that they will simply never be as adaptable, as innovative, or as successful as Company X. Business as usual continues. (Though, come to think of it, if Company X is so great, why did the person who's pushing all this Agile stuff leave there to come work here?)

Adopting Agile practices is seen as an intrinsic goal, not a means to an end

In some cases, organizations stuck in the frameworks trap feel that their Agile journey has been *very* successful. All of their teams have adopted Agile! They're checking the boxes for all the most important Agile rituals, like having daily stand-up meetings, working in sprints, and holding retrospectives! And yet nothing really seems all that different. New cross-functional teams are just as siloed as the old functional teams. Work is delivered in two-week increments, but planned in two-year cycles. The organization has "gone Agile," but business as usual continues.

Although it is appealing to think of Agile as a revolutionary one-size-fits-all solution to the challenges facing modern organizations, simply applying the superficial practices and lingo of Agile without asking "why" all but guarantees that you will find yourself stuck in the frameworks trap. The only way for Agile to meaningfully change the way a group of people works together is for that group to understand its own needs, its own goals, and how its current practices are stopping it from achieving those goals. As shown in Figure 2-2, working together to gain this understanding can help organizations escape the frameworks trap and accomplish meaningful change.

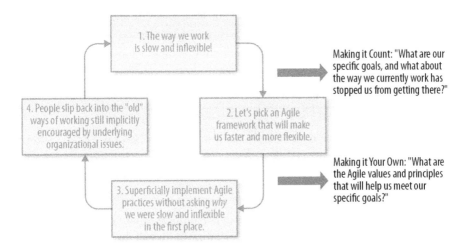

Figure 2-2. Two "off-ramps" for escaping the frameworks trap: making it count, and making it your own.

In this chapter, we look at two "off-ramps" that we can take to escape the frameworks trap: *making it count*, and *making it your own*. Both of these steps serve to anchor Agile practices to Agile values as well as to the specific needs and goals of our organization, thus preventing the frameworks trap from perpetuating an endless untethered cycle of superficial change.

Making It Count: Establishing Your Goals and Challenges

Many companies are drawn to Agile because they see it as a way to be faster and more flexible. But "faster" and "more flexible" are very broad goals that can mean different things to different organizations. What are the specific goals we have with respect to speed and adaptability? How will we know when we are achieving those goals? And, critically, what about the way we are currently working is preventing us from reaching those goals? Without asking these questions, organizations can spend millions of dollars and thousands of productive hours wildly firing silver bullets, without ever asking where they should be aiming in the first place.

Any successful implementation of Agile should begin with a hard, honest look at what is currently working and what is currently not working. If you see

Agile as a trivially demanding operational add-on to your current way of working, the value you derive from it will be just as trivial. Changing practices without challenging the underlying beliefs and expectations that motivate those practices all but guarantees that people will revert to their current state, no matter how many fancy new frameworks you try. Before you implement any specific Agile practices, be prepared to ask and answer the following questions:

- What is the desired future state of our team or organization?
- What is the current state of our team or organization?
- Why do we believe that we have been unable to achieve the desired future state of our team or organization?

These questions are often difficult to answer. Most of us know that we want the way we work to be better, but actually imagining what "better" might look and feel like often means calling into question the deeply held beliefs, expectations, and behaviors that provide us comfort and stability. Indeed, it is not uncommon for people to be very excited about the general idea of positive change but deeply skeptical and resistant to any specific change. In my experience, this skepticism tends to cluster around a few consistent themes:

"We are too hierarchical"

There is no easier way to outright dismiss the possibility of change than to preemptively insist that such change will be scuttled by the powers that be. "We are too hierarchical" is often shorthand for "I am doing my best to work within the parameters and incentives provided by management, and I am afraid of what might happen if those parameters and incentives change." This is a great opportunity to open up a conversation about what aspects of their work your colleagues perceive to be within or outside of their control, and to discuss what kind of change feels possible and desirable within those constraints.

"We are too siloed"

Just about every organization struggles with functional or project-based silos. Agile is often perceived as offering an easy operational solution: reshuffle people from their functional silos into small, cross-functional teams. But these teams can easily become their *own* silos if the underlying cultural issues are not addressed. As we discuss in Chapter 4, there are real and valid reasons why people do not often venture outside the comfort of their immediate teams. Understanding what those reasons are in your organization is critical for thinking through what Agile practices you will deploy to break down organizational silos, and what steps you can take to ensure that cross-functional teams don't become their own silos.

"We are too heavily regulated"

For people working in industries like banking and healthcare, strict regulatory requirements can seem like an impossible obstacle to overcome. But there are still plenty of opportunities to bring Agile principles and values to these industries, even if the specific manifestations of those principles aren't "by the book." Acknowledging the fixed constraints of your organization out of the gate can help you ask "what *can* we do," instead of throwing in the towel as soon as you encounter an Agile practice that would be rendered impossible by regulatory issues.

"We tried to do this before, and it didn't work"

In some cases, there simply is not a widespread belief that change is desirable, or possible. This is particularly true in organizations that have been through the ringer of the frameworks trap multiple times. In cases like this, it is critical to look at *why* past change initiatives have not succeeded— and to do so in a way that is open, honest, and reflective beyond "we picked the wrong framework."

If they are brought to the surface early enough, these common reasons for resisting or doubting change can help you understand exactly what kind of change your organization needs. For example, I have worked with several marketing teams that feel too far removed from their counterparts in product to effect real change for their customers. With this concern brought to light, we have ultimately been able to prioritize tactical steps—some as informal as "email somebody in product and see if they want to grab coffee"—that can contribute to a newfound sense of possibility and momentum. Beyond that, we have been able to model from the outset that giving voice to the challenges we are facing will not impede our Agile journey, but rather direct and accelerate it.

Making It Your Own: Agile Principles and Values to Drive Change

After you've taken the time to articulate the goals of your team or organization, it is time for you to address how Agile might help you to meet those goals. At this point, it can be tempting to jump directly to a framework or set of concrete practices. But doing so misses out on a crucial step: defining the *values* and *principles* of Agile in a way that will resonate for your particular organization. For some organizations, the Agile Manifesto does this quite handily. For other organizations, the Manifesto is not nearly specific enough—as one Agile practitioner I spoke with put it, "Who *wouldn't* say that they value individuals over tools?"

Many Agile practitioners will rightly point out that opening up the core ideas of Agile to any kind of rewording or reframing is a dangerous game. After all, what is to stop people from declaring "Agile" to be whatever they want it to be? What is to stop people from cherry-picking the easiest parts of Agile and ignoring the rest? And what is to stop people from sanitizing the values and principles of Agile so completely that they present no substantive challenge to "business as usual," resulting in the very kind of superficial implementation we discussed earlier in this chapter?

These are important questions and real concerns. But in my experience, asking the question, "How can we frame the values and principles of Agile in a way that will help our team or organization meet its goals?" can bring to light the doubts and disconnects that might drive people to ignore or undermine Agile practices once they are introduced. It gives us a way to engage with potential naysayers while we are still having a high-level discussion about principles and values, helping to create a shared sense of accountability. And most importantly, it helps to mitigate the very real risk that off-the-shelf Agile values and principles will seem vague, unrealistic, or completely irrelevant to our colleagues. As Jodi Leo, an experienced UX practitioner and educator who has worked with organizations like Nava PBC, Apple, Google, and the *New York Times*, told me, "Things always start to go sideways when Agile paradigms are introduced that have absolutely nothing to do with the way that a company is set up to work."

It is important, then, to have a clear sense of whether we are specializing our Agile principles and values to maximize their impact, or sanitizing them to avoid challenging the status quo. To provide an example of the latter, some teams I have worked with have suggested completely removing any references to "collaboration" from their Agile principles and values because they fear that organizational leaders will assume this to mean "more meetings." But this very fear reveals an unmet need to define "collaboration" in a way that will challenge those assumptions. Crafting a specialized principle such as, "We will use our time together to collaboratively shape works in progress, rather than only sharing things that are finished and polished," gives us a chance to frame up the broad idea of collaboration in a way that speaks to the specific needs and goals of our team—which, by this point, we have already had the opportunity to articulate.

Therein lies the critical difference between specializing and sanitizing, as shown in Table 2-1. When we specialize the general values and principles of Agile to make them our own, we are looking to preemptively resolve and address any disconnects that might serve as future excuses for reverting to business as usual. When we sanitize the general values and principles of Agile, we are *already* making excuses for why we cannot meaningfully challenge business as usual.

Table 2-1. Specializing versus sanitizing our Agile principles and values

Specializing	Sanitizing
Incorporating language from existing organizational initiatives that have momentum and buy-in	Superficially combining Agile jargon and existing organizational jargon
Changing particular words or ideas that don't make sense given the way your team or organization operates	Watering down or omitting particular words or ideas that productively challenge the way your team or organization operates
"Will the way I'm framing these principles help my team or organization achieve our specific goals?"	"Will the way I'm framing these principles placate individuals who are fearful of change?"

The chapters that follow break down Agile into three guiding principles that represent my own attempt at capturing the Agile movement in terms that are broad enough to be accessible to all functions and organizations, but specific enough to be actionable. But to be clear, these principles will be much more valuable if you make them your own. Maybe, for example, simply referring to "our customers" is too broad or not applicable for your organization, and you want to change it to "user experience" or "value for our clients." Great! Maybe the "collaboration" you need most immediately is between individuals from specific teams or functions, and you want to codify that in your guiding principles. That's great, too! You have still captured the general ideas of customer centricity and collaboration, and you have done so in a way that will be clear and actionable within your particular organizational context.

Summary: Agile Beyond the Frameworks Trap

Escaping the frameworks trap requires taking two steps *before* you begin looking into specific practices and frameworks:

1. Taking an honest and hard look at what you want your team or organization to look like and what has stopped you from getting there.

2. Adopting (and, if necessary, specializing) a set of guiding Agile principles that you can follow in order to move your team or organization toward your stated goals.

After these two steps are in place, you can commit to a set of practices that will put these principles into action, and work collectively to change these practices if they fall out of synchronization with your guiding principles.

In the next three chapters, we explore three general guiding principles of Agile, some practices that support them, and some common success signals and warning signs that you can use to keep your team or organization on track.

3

Agile Means That We Start with Our Customers

This first guiding principle of Agile is the most important, most challenging, and most-often overlooked. Though Agile is often seen as a set of operational improvements to increase performance or velocity, the heart of any successful

Agile journey is not just how people work together, but rather how they work together to serve their customers.

Truly putting our customers at the center of our work means thinking about their needs, goals, and experiences before we think about the specific thing we are going to deliver to them. This means, as product managers often say, focusing on the *outcomes* we are delivering to our customers before we think about the *outputs* we are going to create. If we can fully understand a customer's entire experience and work backward from there, we can often discover unexpected opportunities, minimize busywork, and give our customers what they want faster than we could before.

Putting customer centricity into practice allows Agile teams to drive better outcomes for their customers and their companies alike, and creates a common language that can extend Agile beyond product and engineering teams. IBM CMO Michelle Peluso described to me how customer centricity has been at the heart of IBM's Agile marketing transformation and how this has helped bring a shared sense of purpose to the entire organization:

> One way I think about Agile is, "Are you bringing the customer front and center? Is the customer experience driving the way you think about work?" That's very much a principle of Design Thinking, as well, which prompts you to think about the most important needs of the customer. The shared principle of customer centricity is one thing that has really aligned our Agile marketing teams with teams that have been through Design Thinking training.

As this example illustrates, customer centricity is one concept that allows us to unite and align around something bigger than our roles, our teams, or our functions. It gives us a shared sense of purpose and a shared bar for success that can cut across toolsets and methodologies. And, at its best, it helps us change our primary goal from "make my boss happy" to "make our customers happy." Lane Goldstone, an experienced Agile practitioner and educator who coaches teams at Capital One, described to me how Agile can help us define "done" by focusing on who really matters:

> Too often, Agile is focused on velocity, and not focused enough on the quality of your outcomes. You can be achieving a high velocity and making nothing that matters. You need to wrap Agile in a structure that helps you

understand that a business stakeholder is not a proxy to the customer. You need to define "done" as being a function of customer value.

Note the critical distinction here between "things that make our business stakeholders happy" and "things that deliver value to our customers." One of the most difficult things about taking a customer-first approach to Agile is acknowledging that these two things are not always aligned and then taking the necessary steps to bring our customers' needs and goals to life for our colleagues and managers.

Some of the practitioners I spoke to prefer specifying that they start with "customer value" or "customer experience" as opposed to simply "our customers." This is one great example of how you might customize these principles with the language and ideas that will resonate the most for your organization. Similarly, if your team or organization primarily serves "users" instead of "customers," you could easily reframe this principle as a function of user centricity, as opposed to customer centricity. If you are focused on growing your business to new audiences, as many marketing departments are, you could indicate that you start with your "current and prospective" customers. The specific language you choose is up to you; what's important is that you *start* by looking beyond the organization itself and toward the people you serve.

Escaping the First Law of Organizational Gravity

At this point, the general idea of customer centricity has become canon for modern businesses. Every organization wants to be, and most claim to be, customer-first, customer-centric, or "customer-obsessed." And yet, most organizations still struggle mightily to keep pace with their customers, and most employees are still much more concerned with what their boss thinks than what their customers think. The hard truth of the matter is that most organizations take precious few steps to encourage the actual work of customer centricity, regardless of what they say in their mission statements and yearly town hall meetings.

The reason for this comes down to the *First Law of Organizational Gravity*: individuals in an organization will avoid customer-facing work if it is not aligned with their day-to-day responsibilities and incentives (Figure 3-1). In other words, organizational leaders can say all they want about customer centricity, but that rhetoric will not translate into action unless individuals throughout the organization see learning from customers as a critical step toward achieving the goals for which they are held accountable.

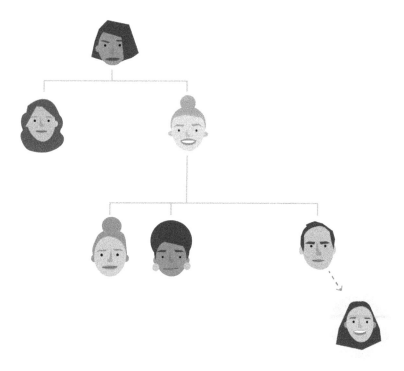

Figure 3-1. The First Law of Organizational Gravity: Individuals in an organization will avoid customer-facing work if it is not aligned with their day-to-day responsibilities and incentives. Note how the org chart clusters away from the one employee directly interacting with a customer at the lower right.

For individuals whose success is measured solely against company-centric goals like timelines and budgets, interacting with customers can be distracting at best and downright dangerous at worst. After all, time spent with customers is time not spent doing the executional work that moves a project tangibly closer to completion. And if your customers complicate your existing plans or challenge your existing assumptions, they may actually slow you down—at least from the company's perspective. For most people in most roles at most organizations, there is simply no immediate reason to prioritize the day-to-day work of customer centricity.

In practice, this often means that the only people within an organization who interact directly with customers are those explicitly tasked with doing so as part of their day-to-day work, such as user experience researchers and customer support agents. And these people are rarely in the room when important decisions are being made. Indeed, it is not at all uncommon for senior leaders in an organization to espouse customer centricity while leaving the actual work of customer centricity to the people farthest from themselves on the org chart—or, as is often the case within marketing functions, to espouse customer centricity while delegating all direct customer research to outside vendors and agencies. This means that the people whose opinions and actions are the most impactful for the overall direction of the business are often the very people who have the least direct knowledge of customer needs and goals.

For any organization seeking to cultivate true customer centricity, this is an enormous roadblock, and one that only compounds itself over time. As leaders become more and more insulated from direct and unmediated interaction with customers, their organizations become ever more poorly equipped to deal with the rapidly accelerating rate of change in customer needs and goals. Even if such organizations succeed in implementing Agile practices, they have not achieved true agility; there is simply too great a distance between decision makers and the customers whose needs and goals should be driving those decisions.

Some organizations have addressed this issue by formally making customer support a shared responsibility across functions and levels. Craig Daniel, VP of product at Drift, described to me how his organization was able to make direct interaction with customers a part of everybody's job, and how this improved the organization's ability to deliver valuable products and features:

When you get people in front of the customer, stuff gets done. People are on the hook. The question is, how do you make that happen? As most organizations grow, they have more and more levels, and most of the people at most of those levels aren't interfacing with customers at all. When you think about it, it really doesn't make any sense.

We talk to our customers every single day. Since we are a chat company, we use chat for many of these interactions. And to make sure that everybody in the organization stays close to our customers, we have an internal chat duty—every single employee works a shift answering customer chats directly. We've also embedded Customer Advocates, who oversee and tri-age these chats, in every single product team.

The results of this approach are always a work in progress. But we've been consistently able to ship both the large and small features that are most important to our customers. We don't need to have meetings to talk about our customers anymore, because knowing our customers is everybody's job. Most of our product managers probably talk to 10 customers a week. Most of our engineers probably talk to at least one customer a week. We don't miss ship dates and deadlines, because we are able to prioritize the work that is most important to our customers and work backward from there.

This example makes a critical point that is often lost in conversations about customer centricity: investing more time in learning directly from customers means that we need to spend less time speculating, socializing, or debating about what our customers really want. Understanding and appreciating the extremely high return on investment that comes from talking to and learning from customers directly is one critical step that organizations can take to overcome the First Law of Organizational Gravity and put customer centricity into practice.

Seeing Speed from the Customer's Point of View

If there is one common misconception about Agile that I've seen have disastrous ramifications for organizations of all shapes and sizes, it is that Agile is only about increasing the speed of execution. As we will see throughout this book, implementing the basic principles of Agile often means taking the time to better understand our customers, share knowledge among our team, and reflect on the way we're working. From the company's point of view, this can look like slowing down. But if we are truly following the principles of Agile, we are measuring speed from the *customer*'s point of view.

What does it mean to see speed from the *customer*'s point of view? It means that the most important question for us to answer is not "How quickly are we doing as much work as possible," but rather "How quickly are we able to deliver value to our customers?" As Mayur Gupta, VP of growth and marketing at Spotify, told me, "agility is measured in your ability to change and evolve based on customer need, not in your speed to execute."

In practice, this means asking, "How can we solve our customers' most important problems as quickly as possible," instead of "What is the most amount of work we can get done in the shortest amount of time?" Product designer and researcher Dr. Anna Harrison described to me a hypothetical scenario that illustrates how customer-centric discipline can run up against executional ambition. Let's imagine that we are working for a company that builds digital waterfowl. We've done our research and discovered that our customers are primarily interested in purchasing ducks. But when we go to our engineering team, they point out that in nearly the same amount of time it takes to deliver a digital duck, they could build a system that gives our users the option to choose from a duck, a goose, or a swan. That seems like a pretty good deal: an incremental increase in time, but a three-times multiple in the waterfowl we can deliver.

Allowing our users to choose between ducks, geese, and swans might seem like added value from our perspective. But from their perspective, we have given them more decisions to make and more work to do. In other words, we have slowed them down. Seeing these other options, they might wonder whether we are truly the best place to buy a digital duck. Or they might just not want to decide in the moment and abandon the transaction altogether.

If we go ahead and launch with a ducks-only product, we might realize later on that we do in fact want to give customers the option to select from a broader range of waterfowl. Or, we might discover that our customers are still primarily interested in buying ducks but are also interested in buying digital pond accessories. Whatever path we wind up taking in the future, we are prioritizing the work that will deliver the most immediate and well-understood value to our customer right now.

Seeing speed from the customer's point of view helps us escape what author and consultant Melissa Perri calls "the build trap (*http://bit.ly/2yi2v7R*)," a common pitfall of Agile in practice (and an inspiration for the frameworks trap described in Chapter 2):

> *The amount of things we produce is no guarantee of a successful company. Building is the easy part of the product development process. Figuring out what to build and how we are going to build it is the hard part. Yet, we only allow ourselves a few days or a week at the beginning of each sprint for designing and speccing this out. We completely neglect research and experimentation in favor of spending more time writing code.*

In other words, if we see Agile as simply a way to do the same things we've always done, only better and faster, we are in no way mitigating the very real risk that our customers might want something different.

Note that the build trap is just as treacherous for folks who are not delivering software products. Rachel Collinson, also known as the Donor Whisperer (*http:// bit.ly/2DYWpzA*), is an Agile practitioner working with nonprofits in the United Kingdom. She described to me how the Agile principle of customer centricity stands to transform that sector as well:

> What charities often do is put together a long research report, spend ages working with a designer, launch it, publish it, and then work with PR to get it out into the world. They expect that report to have a huge impact, and often it doesn't. But accomplishing a charity's underlying goals isn't just about getting more organized and getting out ahead of the deadlines; it's about asking, "Do we need the report at all?" It's about using user-centered design principles to say, "What problem are we trying to solve? Who is this for, what are their needs?"

> The same thing is true when it comes to fundraising. There is an increasing hysteria in the media about the methods charities use to raise funds, and questions about how effective charities are, whether they exist at all, should they be looking at root causes or should they just be handing food to hungry people. Rather than saying, "Maybe we should do fundraising a new way," many nonprofits are doubling down on the old way, which is to write an extremely guilt-provoking letter and send it to as many people as possible. These organizations spend months agonizing over the text, and getting the photos right, and designing it perfectly. Then they send the direct mail and they analyze the results and say, "Oh, that didn't do as well as we hoped." But from a donor's perspective, direct mail is often a fundamentally bad experience, regardless of how much time and effort a nonprofit puts into choosing the photos and writing the text.

> What I'm trying to do now is just listen closely to donors and ask those bigger questions about how we can align what we do with their goals and needs. Then I test an MVC (Minimum Viable Campaign) with them and scale up, polish, and launch only if the response is good. It's a tough sell, but I know it's the only thing that's going to work.

As this story illustrates, organizations of all kinds have a tendency to default to what they've done in the past—even if it is not what their customers (or in this case, donors) really want. In cases like this, operational "speed" is ultimately irrelevant. Thus, it is critical to put an explicit commitment to customer centricity at the heart of any Agile journey.

Beyond "Working Software"

The Agile Manifesto has its own way of reframing speed as a function of customer value:

Working software over comprehensive documentation

Many critics of Agile approaches have misinterpreted this as an anarchistic decree that all documentation be torn up and discarded forever. But the intent behind this statement of values is actually pretty straightforward: *focus on the things that deliver immediate value to your customers.* Comprehensive documentation can feel like progress, but until you have something that your customers can actually use, you haven't made much progress at all.

The fact that the Agile Manifesto specifies "working software" has also contributed to the misconception that Agile is only for software developers and cannot be extended to other parts of an organization. But, as Table 3-1 indicates, every kind of product or deliverable has its equivalent of "working software"— something that your customers can interact with directly to ascertain whether or not it is meeting their needs and goals.

Table 3-1. "Working software" versus "comprehensive documentation" for different types of deliverables

Type of deliverable	"Working software"	"Comprehensive documentation"
Software product	"Minimum Viable Product" or functional prototype	Product specification or documentation
Marketing campaign	Social media message tests	Yearly marketing plan
Book	Sample chapter	Proposal
Home design	VR walkthrough	Blueprint
Cake	Test bake	Recipe
Presentation	Rough slides	Text outline

When we take this broader approach to defining "working software," we are able to spend less time on intermediate states that deliver no real value to our customers. Instead, we are compelled to ask, "What can we put together that our customer can actually use, and that we can actually learn from?" In the Lean Startup world, this approach is often called Minimum Viable Product (MVP), but it can be used for developing much more than products.

To use a common example, imagine that you are tasked with putting together a PowerPoint presentation for your colleagues. Your first instinct might be to fire up Word and begin meticulously constructing a long, comprehensive outline. A week later, you show the outline to a few people to get their feedback. The bullet points make sense, and the structure of the information seems pretty logical. You breathe a sigh of relief. Now it's just a matter of taking the outline and turning it into slides.

The night before the presentation, you begin transferring your outline over into slides—and realize very quickly that your blocks of meticulously constructed text do not make for a visually compelling slide deck. But the presentation is tomorrow, and you're running out of time, so it will have to do. The next day, you connect your laptop to the conference room TV screen and fire up your presentation. As you look out over a conference table full of scrunched-up faces trying to decipher blocks of pixelated text, it suddenly dawns on you: from your audience's point of view, that big meticulous outline means nothing. The comprehensive document to which you devoted the majority of your time and energy may have given you a sense of progress and accomplishment, but it was dangerously disconnected from what your audience would actually experience.

Now imagine if you had started with a working-software approach. Rather than spending a week creating a meticulous and detailed outline, you could have given yourself a day or two to put together a draft slide deck, visuals and all. Rather than asking your colleagues to read several pages of dense text in a format that your audience would never see, you could have walked your colleagues through that draft and learned from their reactions. Any scrunched faces or furrowed brows could have been valuable and actionable feedback, not signs of a failure already in progress. In other words, if you had started by getting as close as possible to the experience you were creating for your audience, you would have been in a much better position to understand and improve that experience before it was too late.

Starting with our customers (or audience) and working backward also helps us understand parts of the customer experience that might fall outside the immediate scope of our working software. Even the most well-crafted presentation, for example, can fall flat if it is delivered in a sad windowless room or if the screen in that sad windowless room requires an adaptor that nobody can find. Thinking through these other contextual issues, captured in Table 3-2, can help us understand how our working software fits into the overall customer experience, and take steps to improve that experience that we might not have thought about previously.

Table 3-2. Expanding working software to include other parts of the customer experience

Type of deliverable	Other parts of customer experience to consider	Working software	Comprehensive documentation
Software product	Installation/onboarding, other software used at the same time	MVP or functional prototype	Product specification or documentation
Marketing campaign	Personalization, overall platform experience	Social media message tests	Yearly marketing plan
Book	Paper versus digital edition, typeface	Sample chapter	Proposal
Home design	Neighborhood, finishes and accessories	VR walkthrough	Blueprint
Cake	Serving tray, accompanying beverage	Test bake	Recipe
Presentation	Room, technical setup	Rough slides	Outline

Taking this broader, customer experience–first approach can often help us identify unexpected areas to grow our business. One of my favorite examples of this comes from Fender Musical Instruments, who zoomed out from their product offerings to grow their business by understanding the entire experience around buying and learning to play a guitar. In an interview with *Forbes* (*http://bit.ly/2ydVmpf*), Fender CEO Andy Mooney described the user research that compelled Fender to create its Fender Play instructional platform for beginner guitarists:

About two years ago we did a lot of research about new guitar buyers. We were hungry for data and there wasn't much available. We found that 45% of all the guitars we sell every year go to first-time players. That was much higher than we imagined. Ninety percent of those first-time players abandoned the instrument in the first 12 months—if not the first 90 days—but the 10% that didn't tend to commit to the instrument for life and own multiple guitars and multiple amps.

> *...The last thing we found was that new buyers spend four times as much on lessons as they do on equipment. So that shaped a number of things. It shaped the commitment we made to Fender Play because we felt there was an independent business opportunity available to us that we'd never considered before because the trend in learning was moving online.*

This example illustrates how a truly Agile approach, by any name, must begin with a clear and holistic understanding of the entire customer experience. This understanding allowed a legacy business to make a big move in a challenging industry, and Fender is currently growing at a faster rate than the musical instrument business overall.

Thinking holistically about the customer experience also gives us a way to recontextualize a few well-known quotes that are often cited to defend a general lack of customer-centric practices. First, there is Steve Jobs in a 1998 interview with *Business Week* claiming that "A lot of times, people don't know what they want until you show it to them." And then there is Henry Ford's famous, if likely apocryphal, declaration[1] that "If I had asked people what they wanted, they would have said faster horses."

At first glance, these quotes seem to tell a similar story: certain innovations—like, say, the iPhone and the automobile—are so radical, so transformative, so truly and profoundly *new*, that customers would never be able to imagine them, let alone ask for them. But, as any user researcher would be quick to tell you, asking customers what they want is not the same thing as learning from customers. Taking a broader view of the customer experience is exactly what allows us to see beyond narrow, transactional questions like, "How fast do you want your horse to be," "What features do you want on your flip phone," or, to return to the Fender example, "What color guitar would you be most likely to purchase?"

Even if we are to take these two famous quotes at face value, neither is actually a call against customer centricity. In fact, the respective successes of both the automobile and the iPhone speak to how a broader understanding of customers' needs and goals can uncover entirely new solutions.

---

1 The *Harvard Business Review* reported in 2011 that (*http://bit.ly/2O3ZwL2*) there is no evidence that Ford ever actually uttered these words.

Agile Practice Deep Dive: Working in Sprints

If the entire universe of Agile methodologies could be summarized by a single practice, it is that of working in *time-boxed iterations*, often referred to as *sprints*. In each sprint, a team agrees to deliver some kind of working software in a short, finite, and agreed-upon timeframe. The team then gathers feedback on the working software it has produced, and incorporates that feedback into the next round of work. As we discussed earlier in this chapter, working software does not need to be actual software; it is simply something that replicates as closely as possible the customer experience you are seeking to create.

Even as an abstract thought exercise, sprints are an incredibly powerful tool. Imagine, in the middle of a six-month project, being forced to decide what you would actually release to your customers if you had only two weeks to work. Would you complete and polish a single part of what you initially planned to deliver? Or, would you try to create a smaller and potentially less-polished version of the whole thing? In either case, you are forced to ask an important and incredibly difficult question: if we only have a small amount of time in which to actually deliver something to our customers, *what do we deliver?*

This question, in turn, often opens up several adjacent cans of worms. How do we break apart our grand plans into more approachable pieces? How can we accurately estimate what we can actually get done in two weeks? How do we know what our customers actually want? And have we even taken the time to really define who our customers are in the first place?

Many of the practices within specific Agile methodologies and frameworks are designed to answer these very questions. But, for many teams and organizations approaching Agile for the first time, simply asking these questions is enough to bring previously uninterrogated assumptions into the light. And, because sprints are usually quite short, committing to working in this way means that we must ask these questions regularly and be prepared for our answers to change. As shown in Figure 3-2, this gives us the opportunity to frequently adjust both the work we do and the way we work to better reflect the fast-changing needs of our customers.

When I began introducing the practice of working in sprints to product teams, I found that most of the pushback I received was not actually about the relatively short duration of each sprint. Instead, it was about the idea that each sprint should involve getting feedback from customers. "If we have only two weeks to work," I would often hear, "how are we supposed to make time to get feedback from customers?"

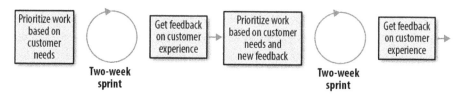

Figure 3-2. Using Agile sprints to incorporate customer feedback at regular intervals.

It was these conversations that helped me begin to understand the First Law of Organizational Gravity described earlier in this chapter. In far too many organizations, directly interacting with customers is simply not seen as an important or valuable use of time. Unfortunately, the idea that Agile is a means to get more work done in less time often reinforces this belief. After all, if our goal is simply to get more work done, why would we waste our time talking to customers when we could be spending that time making more stuff?

The answer, of course, is that our customers are the people who ultimately decide whether the stuff we're making is successful. It is here where the relationship between principles and practices becomes critically important. "Work in two-week cycles called sprints" is not, and should not be, a principle or a value. Simply breaking down work into two-week chunks, as shown in Figure 3-3, does not mean that we are following our Agile principles and values. If anything, it allows us to superficially check the "doing Agile" box while only growing farther removed from our customers and more resistant to change.

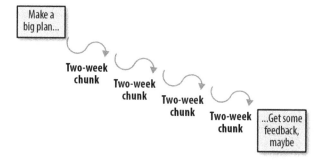

Figure 3-3. Breaking a big plan into two-week chunks—which is not the same thing as working in sprints!

If we break down a large work plan into two-week chunks that do not include our customers, we are not working in sprints at all; we are, instead, simply slapping an Agile veneer on business as usual.

If you choose to pursue working in sprints, here are a few tips to make sure that you are staying true to our first guiding principle of Agile:

Make customer feedback a required part of every cycle

The easiest way to align Agile sprints with your goal of customer centricity is simply to make sure that gathering customer feedback is an essential and unskippable part of every cycle. This might seem daunting at first, but it is one of many ways that you can use the time constraints of a sprint in your favor. Prioritizing time spent with customers reinforces the value of this time and helps to avoid situations in which any time not spent "producing" is seen as wasteful.

Find your own definition of working software

What is it that you will deliver and test at the end of each cycle? And how will it help you to better understand the entire customer experience toward which you are working? Depending on the kind of work your team does, the answers to these questions might be very different. Take the time to discuss them upfront so that you don't find yourself operating under misaligned assumptions about what "done" means.

Be ready to throw away the work that you just did

One of the other advantages to working in sprints is that you minimize sunk cost if you've begun building something that you learn does not meet the needs of your customers. This can be a tough pill to swallow, but if you get out ahead of these conversations, it can be an important step toward getting people to understand that their work is only as valuable to the organization as it is to your customers. When people are comfortable discarding the work from their previous sprint, it shows that they are valuing customer learning over speed of production—a surefire sign that you are on the right track.

Don't become paralyzed by the details

I have worked with several teams that were initially unable to commit to working in sprints because they could not agree upon how long each sprint should be or how to estimate the work that would be delivered in each sprint. These are important questions to ask, but the right answers are unlikely to present themselves without a fair amount of trial and error, and are likely to change over time regardless. Pick a place to start, and make it clear that there will be plenty of opportunities to adjust course if things are not going as planned (we discuss this at greater length in Chapter 5).

As always, staying firmly grounded in your Agile principles will help to guide you to a meaningful implementation of this and all Agile practices. Jennifer Katz, senior director of brand culture at USA and SyFy networks, described to me how taking a principles-first approach to Agile sprints can be equally valuable for large and subjective projects such as show launches:

> Scrum training was very eye-opening for us, and made it clear that there was a lot we could take from the practice and incorporate into our business for a more fluid day-to-day workflow. The way software developers do it, you can be constantly producing code and getting instant feedback. For us, the feedback cycle has traditionally been very different. You do all of this work leading up to a show launching, and it's not until that show premieres that you really see if all the work put into the campaign did its job and brought viewers in.
>
> We were excited to learn about a more iterative approach so that we could learn faster, fail quicker, and bring our learnings back to the team. And that iterative approach feels much truer to our audience. People are no longer just watching linearly—our viewers are flocking to different channels in new and nonlinear ways, constantly. Gone are the days when you could just create a 30-second spot and then retrofit it to a bunch of different platforms. You need to think about it holistically, from the viewer's perspective and experience and where they want to go to consume content. That's been the big learning curve for us—getting everybody here to think a little differently. And part of that is creating a more flexible working system.
>
> One thing we've learned is that you need to customize that system for the needs of your team and organization. The group of us that went through the training looked at the philosophies and the practices of Agile and said, "What works for our environment? Knowing that there are a lot of layers, there are processes that cannot be moved, how do we build and work around that in a way that still lends itself to the working practice of Agile?" A lot of it came down to getting people comfortable with sharing things in

rough-draft form. Instead of waiting to too far down the line to internally share the campaign materials for approval, get it to key decision makers earlier, more often, and faster, so you aren't sitting there doing all of this work and then having to go back and do it all again.

As this story illustrates, the foundational ideas behind sprint-based work are very much applicable beyond the world of software development. Even if we are working on projects that involve long timeframes and fixed schedules, we can always look for ways to imagine the customer experience more holistically, and gather feedback about this experience more regularly.

Quick Wins to Put This Principle into Practice

Here are some steps that different teams can take to begin putting our Agile guiding principle of customer centricity into practice:

For marketing teams, you could try...

...breaking the habit of delivering customer insights in the form of large PowerPoint decks and delivering smaller and timelier customer insights more often.

...getting out of the building and interacting with customers directly, even if it is just a matter of talking to somebody on a street corner or at a coffee shop.

For sales teams, you could try...

...sending a quick email to your counterparts in product or marketing that captures insights from a failed customer call or lost sale, to share your understanding of evolving customer needs.

For executives, you could try...

...taking a direct and unmediated look at support channels and customer feedback to better understand the real-world needs and goals of your customers.

...publicly recognizing and rewarding the actual work of customer centricity in addition to the rhetoric of "customer centricity."

For product and engineering teams, you could try...

...walking through real-world use of your product with actual customers as part of each and every development cycle.

...starting every new product or feature idea with a clear description of the value it will provide to your customers.

For an entire Agile organization, you could try...

...getting in the habit of using your own products or services (a practice sometimes called "eating your own dog food" or "dogfooding") to better understand the overall customer experience.

YOU MIGHT BE ON THE RIGHT TRACK IF:

Your customers are surprising you

Starting with our customers means opening ourselves up to hearing things we didn't expect. When an organization is truly following this first guiding principle of Agile, it often hears things from its customers that are surprising, inconvenient, or outright shocking. Although this can be uncomfortable, it is also a reliable sign that you are breaking the patterns of company centricity and uncovering new opportunities for customer-driven growth.

To keep the momentum going around this, you might want to:

- Share new and surprising customer insights as widely as you can, and ask counterparts from different parts of the business what the ramifications of these insights might be for them.

- Frame surprising customer feedback as a matter of opportunity, and initiate conversations about new and exciting ways to help customers meet their needs and goals.

- Create and share quick mockups or prototypes of ways in which you could incorporate the new information you are receiving from your customers into your existing products or projects.

Organizational and team leaders are asking customer-centric questions in meetings

One of the many ways that organizational leaders often accidentally undermine Agile principles is to continue asking only company-centric questions, such as "Are we on time and on budget?" and "Has your manager approved this?" as opposed to customer-centric questions, such as "How do our customers feel about this change to the product?" One immediate and powerful sign that you're on the right track is that leaders are asking customer-centric questions or, even better, referring directly to customer quotes and insights.

To keep the momentum going around this, you might want to:

- Formalize customer-centric questions as part of your meeting agendas.
- Encourage team and organizational leaders to participate more directly in customer research.
- Invite more people from different parts of the organization to join the meetings where these questions are being asked.

You are incorporating customer feedback into every step of your process, from initial idea through execution

Solving for customer centricity is sometimes easier at the beginning of a given project before executional deadlines come into play. It is not uncommon, for example, that marketing campaigns begin with customer insights that are long-forgotten by the time that agency creatives begin coming up with concepts. One clear sign that you're on the right track is that you are incorporating customer feedback into *every* stage of work, from initial idea through execution.

To keep the momentum going around this, you might want to:

- Make customer feedback an integral part of any design review process.
- Get in the habit of asking vendors, agency partners, and internal creatives if they have had a chance to get feedback from customers.
- Create an "insights brief" that can follow a project through its entire life cycle and keep customer understanding front-of-mind.

YOU MIGHT BE GOING ASTRAY IF:

Direct interaction with customers is seen as low-status drudgery—or is outsourced

As we discussed earlier in this chapter, it is extremely difficult for organizations to cultivate true customer centricity if direct interaction with customers is seen as low-status work or outsourced entirely to external agencies and vendors. If people in the organization are generally avoiding or dismissing direct interaction with customers, you have some work to do.

If this is happening, you might want to:

- Simply acknowledge that customer-facing work is seen as low-status in your organization and have a candid conversation with your colleagues about why this is and how you can address it.

- Encourage team and organizational leaders to explicitly acknowledge the value of directly customer-facing work—or, better yet, to visibly participate in that work.

- Create a "shift" system by which everybody in the organization handles a customer-facing task like customer support. (Depending on how built-out your customer support function is, this might involve "pairing" with trained customer support experts.)

New product or service ideas are framed as "innovations" or "disruptions"

I am deeply skeptical of the words "innovation" and "disruption" for many reasons, but most of all because they are deeply company-centric language. Customers choose the experiences that best meet their needs and goals, not the most "innovative" or "disruptive." Although many organizations are drawn to Agile because they see it as a way to keep pace with new technologies, it is critical to establish the ultimate goal of any Agile journey as better serving customers, not as becoming an "innovative" organization.

If this is happening, you might want to:

- Ban the "i"-word and the "d"-word from your organization, and insist that any new ideas are presented through the lens of customer needs and goals.

- Get in the habit of asking what customer need or goal these innovative new ideas are actually addressing.

- Conduct some quick qualitative research to get a sense for whether an innovative product or service idea is relevant to your customers.

The only customer feedback that travels through the organization is positive customer feedback

When organizations have adopted the practices but not the principle of customer centricity, they often (mis)use customer feedback as a way to selectively validate and support the things that the company already wants to do. If the only customer feedback you're seeing is positive feedback—or if any negative feedback is being dismissed as "outside of our target customer" or "just a bunch of trolls," your organization might be talking to customers, but it is certainly not listening.

If this is happening, you might want to:

- Create a lightweight template for customer feedback sessions that includes room for unexpected, negative, or contradictory information.

- Ask to see the raw transcripts or videos of customer interviews, and look for things that are new and/or surprising.

- Show your customers multiple versions of things and ask which they prefer so that the feedback you receive is neither purely "positive" nor purely "negative," but instead indicates directional preference.

The progress of your Agile journey is measured only by operational metrics like adoption or velocity

As we discussed earlier in this chapter, Agile is designed to increase the speed at which we can deliver valuable solutions to our customers—not the speed at which we can produce the same old things we've always produced. If the success of your Agile journey is being measured only by operational metrics, without tracking customer-facing success in tandem, you are likely to find yourself stuck in the build trap, working ever harder to make things that have little impact on your customer or your business.

If this is happening, you might want to:

- Use customer satisfaction metrics, along with operational metrics, to measure the success of your Agile initiatives.

- Have a conversation with organizational leaders about seeing speed from the customer's point of view, and make sure they understand that solving customer needs faster might actually feel like slowing down the speed of outputs.

- Reserve a day, a few days, or even a week to hit "pause" on production and focus exclusively on customer research and interaction. This sends a clear message that you are truly putting your customers first, and putting their needs and goals ahead of operational optimization.

Summary: Customers First!

In theory, customer centricity is a no-brainer. In practice, however, it often means making substantial changes to the way we work and at times challenging some deeply entrenched assumptions about what we are doing and why. For these reasons and many more, it is important that we *start* with our customers, to make as much room as possible for their fast-changing needs and goals to guide both what we create and how we create it.

In the chapters that follow, we discuss two more guiding principles of Agile that can help us turn the things we learn from our customers into timely and meaningful solutions: collaborating early and often, and planning for uncertainty.

4

Agile Means That We Collaborate Early and Often

The idea of working in small, cross-functional teams is central to several Agile methodologies. But, as with many other Agile practices, it is much easier to approach this as an operational change than as a cultural change. In far too many cases, organizations simply add a few dotted lines to the org chart or implement an open-office plan without really thinking through why cross-functional collaboration is valuable to the organization and its customers, and what has impeded it in the past.

And therein lies the greatest challenge of this guiding principle: just because people are on a team together or in a meeting together does not necessarily mean that they are *collaborating*. True collaboration requires openness, vulnerability, and the willingness to share ownership over ideas. It requires asking a question before you know the answer and being prepared to receive an answer you did not expect. It is something that does not come easily for most organizations, no matter how much time people spend in meetings.

This is why our second guiding principle is to collaborate *early and often*, both within and beyond our teams. Collaborating early means that we collaborate during upfront strategic conversations as well as downstream tactical ones, opening up the possibility of discovering new and unseen solutions. Collaborating often means that we continue these conversations throughout the process of creating and delivering, ensuring that strategy and tactics remain aligned and giving us more opportunities to adjust course as needed.

For organizations in which collaboration between particular groups is a well-understood problem, describing the specific silos across which we need to work more closely is one way to specialize this principle for your particular needs. You might want to say, for example, "We collaborate across functional roles," or "We collaborate across product teams." For some organizations and teams, it might also be worth explicitly denoting what we mean by collaboration. For example, "We collaborate early and often by sharing works-in-progress and asking questions before we know the answer." Again, it is important for you to find the framing that speaks most directly to your own organization's needs and goals.

Escaping the Second Law of Organizational Gravity

At times, the lack of connection and collaboration in even the most well-intentioned organizations can seem bewildering. Even when collaboration is codified in a company's mission statement or operating principles, people still tend to default to working only with the people in their immediate orbit.

I call this the *Second Law of Organizational Gravity* (Figure 4-1): individuals in an organization will prioritize the work that they can complete most easily within the comfort of their own team or silo. As with all our laws of organizational gravity, this is a force that is rarely named or seen in the open, but one that has an enormous impact on the way that modern organizations work.

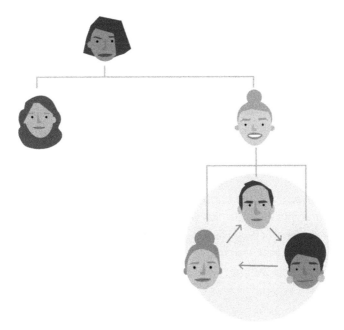

Figure 4-1. The Second Law of Organizational Gravity: Individuals in an organization will prioritize the work that they can complete most easily within the comfort of their own team or silo. Note how the gravitational field at the lower right pulls members of a single team closer to each other and farther away from their colleagues elsewhere in the organization.

The reasons why individuals might choose to prioritize the work that requires the least support from outside their team or silo are not terribly difficult to grasp. Imagine that you are on the hook for delivering something that your boss has demanded be completely finished by a certain date at a certain time. You know that your deliverable would be stronger if you got input from different teams—but you also know that the people on those teams likely have their own priorities, their own objectives, and their own deadlines to worry about. Even worse, they might undermine your work—or take credit for your work if it succeeds! Simply put, venturing outside of your own team or silo is risky, and minimizing risk is a successful strategy in most modern organizations.

In many ways, Agile is designed to harness the power of this gravitational force by creating empowered, autonomous, and cross-functional teams. If your immediate team consists of *everybody* whose work is required to create a successful customer experience, the work that is most important to your customers is more likely to be prioritized. In practice, however, it is rarely either possible or advisable for a team to actually include every single person whose work touches a given product or project. And so the need to create a culture of collaboration across teams and silos persists even when an organization has formally reorganized itself into small, cross-functional teams.

It is often when organizations facilitate collaboration across their most disconnected and far-flung teams that they are able to achieve the most impressive results. Jodi Leo, an experienced UX practitioner and educator who has worked with organizations like Nava PBC, Apple, Google, and the *New York Times*, described to me how a financial services company was able to meet an impossible-seeming deadline by connecting its product and compliance teams:

> *In November of 2014, we had the opportunity to create one of the first apps for the Apple Watch, which would be featured in Tim Cook's keynote. That's not the kind of opportunity you can pass up. But this seemed like a nearly impossible task—we had 120 days to create something for a brand-new platform, and we didn't even have an app for the iPhone yet. The message from executives was clear: we don't care what mountains you need to move, we want you to make this happen.*
>
> *Miraculously, we got it done on time—and, beyond that, it was a great bonding experience for everybody involved. One main reason for this is that we were able to move a mountain that has not been moved before or since: we had compliance officers actually sitting on the floor with us. In the past, compliance had always been seen as the rarified team who said "no" and made our jobs more difficult at the last minute. But our relationship with them was very different when they were actually part of the team. They were there with us reviewing designs before we sent them to code, and about 50% of the time they would be able to find a workaround that maintained the integrity of the user experience. Having them there with us made such a big difference, and made such a clear case for the importance of collaboration.*

This example illustrates just how critical it is that we collaborate *early and often* across even the most entrenched and calcified silos in our organization. When we engage people such as lawyers and compliance officers early enough, we have the opportunity to explore multiple solutions *before* we have finalized something to which they can only say "yes" or "no." This allows us to better understand and internalize the underlying rules and regulations that guide their decisions, which in turn minimizes both the time needed for costly regulatory review and the time needed to rework anything that fails such review. This is one example of how time invested in collaboration across functions and teams can yield tremendous long-term returns.

Moving from a Report and Critique Culture to a Collaborative Culture

In far too many cases, people interested in bringing Agile to their teams or organizations feel that increasing collaboration is not possible without a formal reorganization, whether it is the reshuffling of individuals from functional teams into cross-functional teams, or the establishment of a multitiered cross-functional system that operates on the "squad," "tribe," "chapter," and "guild" level (often called the "Spotify model"). Mayur Gupta, VP of growth and marketing at Spotify, described to me how even the Spotify model is less a question of org charts, and more a question of culture:

> When people refer to the Spotify model, they're usually talking about guilds, tribes, and chapters. But those are just rituals. I don't believe that you break down barriers by changing reporting lines. When you have a truly cross-functional team, reporting lines become irrelevant. The way you run the business, and the way you solve problems, inherently has to be done cross-functionally.
>
> As you keep going through your life and career, you realize that what truly drives these changes is the culture. That to me is paramount—the culture of your organization. The culture of how you grow individuals, how you inspire your employee base, how you recognize your employee base. That culture becomes truly cross-functional when you are agnostic of where you sit, and when you start to recognize collaboration as opposed to individual heroism. At the end of the day we all want to be recognized for the work we do. If recognition operates in silos, or is only given to individuals, then that's how individuals will seek recognition. We need to recognize teamwork and we need to acknowledge teamwork.

Even for Spotify itself, a successful implementation of the Spotify model has less to do with the specifics of the frameworks and reporting structures the company has adopted, and more to do with the culture that it has cultivated. For many organizations, there is a fundamental—if often unspoken—belief that working together is simply a waste of time and efficiency. Even when these organizations adopt Agile practices, they have a difficult time imagining what a more collaborative culture might look like beyond "more meetings." For these organizations, a fundamental cultural shift must take place: the shift from a *report-and-critique* culture to a *collaborative* culture.

A report-and-critique culture is one in which teams and functions do their own work and then hold meetings to tell other teams about that work. Those teams, in turn, are only able to offer inputs on something that has already been completed, resulting in contributions that feel more like critique than collaboration. For many organizations, this is the sum total of what "meetings" across teams and functions represent. Table 4-1 demonstrates how a report-and-critique culture is very different from a truly collaborative, Agile culture.

Table 4-1. Report-and-critique culture versus collaborative Agile culture

Report-and-critique culture	Collaborative Agile culture
Meetings are a chance to present work that has already been completed	Meetings are a chance to share ideas and make decisions about works in progress
Interaction with people from other teams or functions is inefficient and to be avoided unless there is an immediate tactical dependency to be resolved	Interaction with people from other teams or functions is seen as a way to get out ahead of potential future dependencies and conflicts
Each team has distinct—and at times conflicting—goals	Each team's goals are aligned under overall company and customer goals
Team divisions and chains of command are absolute and unchanging	Team divisions and chains of command can be reorganized temporarily around project needs

Some organizations develop a report-and-critique culture as a reaction to misaligned goals and incentives between teams. For example, one team might be held accountable for the number of new customers acquired through marketing efforts, while another team is held accountable for the average revenue earned per customer. As the first team casts a wide net and brings in low-value customers, the second team's success metric suffers. The resulting mistrust stifles collaboration and makes it all too easy for either team to blame the other if they fail to reach their respective goals.

More commonly, a report-and-critique culture emerges when individuals only reach out across teams and silos when there is an immediate, tactical dependency to be resolved. This perpetuates the belief that other teams exist only to derail or complicate your own team's work, leaving ample room for misunderstanding and little room for true collaboration.

Finally, a report-and-critique culture is often a simple product of the fact that people will generally prefer to share things that are finished, polished, and impressive—especially when sharing with people who might not be immediately familiar with the quality of their day-to-day work.

Shifting from a report-and-critique culture to a collaborative culture is no easy feat and, as with the adoption of Agile principles in general, more of an ongoing journey than a finite transformation. But at its heart, this shift involves giving people the opportunity to experience collaboration as something that will help them achieve their goals, not something that will delay or derail them in achieving those goals. Often, the best way to accelerate this shift is simply to begin reaching out to people from other parts of your organization and learning more about their particular goals and objectives—*before* you need something from them or have something finished and polished to share with them. Alan Bunce, a consultant and former marketing leader at organizations like IBM and Salesforce.com, described to me how he was able to create a more collaborative culture by encouraging one-on-one relationships between individuals across functions and silos:

> At one company where I worked, we had these weekly or biweekly product marketing and product management meetings. All 10 of our product managers, and all six of our product marketers, attended every meeting. There was always an agenda, and it was always useless. These meetings were torture, and you never really got anything out of them.
>
> I try to avoid having those big meetings where there's an agenda and somebody presents. At the next company where I worked, I agreed with my counterpart, the head of product management, that what we really needed was to develop strong one-on-one relationships between product marketers and product managers. You shouldn't need to wait for the next meeting. You're talking to each other informally all the time.

Note that many practitioners I have spoken to have a very different perspective about meetings without formal agendas. This, again, illustrates how different teams and organizations will need to take different steps to move toward a truly collaborative culture. If, for example, your team is struggling with disorganized meetings that don't offer any clear value, using formalized agendas to structure space for collaborative decision making might be an important step forward. If you are working in an organization in which formal agendas are reinforcing the perception that something must be finished and polished before it can be shared, you might take a very different approach.

In either case, there are always opportunities to look beyond transactional and structured meetings and create more space for informal communication. It is often through these conversations that individuals from different teams discover opportunities to work together toward a shared set of goals.

The Room Where It Happens

Many organizations seek to instill the Agile value of collaboration by creating open and flexible floorplans, sometimes called *Agile zones* or, in some cases, *Agile cities*. As a rule, you need not spend too much time in one of these zones to determine whether its energy matches its title. Some Agile zones buzz with interaction, creativity, and collaboration. Others are tense, stifled, and permeated by the palpable discomfort of individuals desperately vying for any crumbs of personal space.

The difference has less to do with the spaces themselves, and more to do with the teams that inhabit them. For teams that are used to working in a synchronous, face-to-face way, an open Agile zone can be an ideal working environment. But if a team communicates primarily via asynchronous email threads, Google Docs comments, and PowerPoint presentations, an open Agile zone is at best irrelevant and at worst enormously distracting.

These asynchronous methods of communication have become the default for many teams, including teams that are entirely colocated. In many cases, working this way just seems easier; shooting off a quick email or tagging someone in a Google Docs thread doesn't take much time at all, and it certainly feels like a less onerous task than throwing yet another meeting on people's already-packed calendars. And yet, each of these actions incurs a cascading cost of time and attention that is often difficult to see and measure. Sure, it does not take long to add a few more people to an email thread or to pop a few comments in a document to show that you're paying attention. But for the people receiving those emails and comments, this can add up to a mountain of ambiguously prioritized busywork detached from clear goals and outcomes.

This dynamic often results in a lot of time being lost without a lot of decisions being made. And when you're on an email thread with 20 other people, it can be difficult to know what a "decision" even is. Does everybody need to agree? Is the lack of feedback an implicit sign of approval? This lack of clarity often makes it particularly difficult for a team to move forward with any kind of work that requires input from multiple people.

When I started researching this book, I was bowled over by a brief case study in Scott Brinker's Chief Marketing Technologist blog about Coca-Cola applying Agile principles to its 2006 FIFA World Cup campaign (and refining and extending their approach in subsequent World Cup campaigns). To summarize, Coca-Cola was developing the campaign with two different agencies, one for design and one for technical implementation. These two agencies had once been part of the same agency and did not enjoy a particularly harmonious working relationship. To get things moving, the folks at Coca-Cola invited representatives from these agencies to sit in a room together and develop a plan collaboratively. The conversations themselves were not always easy, but the outcome was fairly miraculous: a giant global ad campaign finished just ahead of schedule. As they refined their Agile approach for 2010 and 2014, they were able to deliver increasingly sophisticated campaigns well ahead of schedule.

I had the chance to chat with Thomas Stubbs, who led Coca-Cola through that particular Agile initiative and continues to push the organization toward embracing more Agile ways of working. He described to me how taking this "hothouse" approach has helped his teams collaborate more closely and hit their deadlines:

> We've operated under the very simple principle that we're not going to communicate over email and PowerPoint presentation; we're going to put the designers and the technical folks into a room with the business owners and let them do their work. I've always called it a "hothouse" approach, and I've been using it since before I knew anything about Agile. Putting the right people together, we are able to make decisions and make progress really fast.
>
> It's also much harder to create negative working relationships when you sit in the room with someone and figure something out. There are boundaries of civility that generally apply to how you will interact with the person who is sitting across from you. Email, meanwhile, can become a passive-aggressive medium when misused—making it possibly the worst tool for

Agile ever invented. The wrong people can be copied, and people who don't need to be copied are sometimes copied. And even the people who should be copied get a lot of things they don't need to see. Beyond that, people's ability to perceive and deliver content and context is challenged over email. In situations where we need to make decisions and move fast, PowerPoint and email slow progress.

I don't think there's a neat formula for who should be in the room. Decision makers should be there, and team leaders trusted by the people who aren't in the room, for sure. There's also certainly a number at which gathering people in the same room becomes unwieldy and doesn't work so much anymore. I don't know what that number is, but when you start getting north of 10, you've got enough conversations and chaos in a small place to make things difficult. We did have it north of 10 for the Brazil World Cup campaign—which, in retrospect, was probably too many. But we still made it work. And we still managed to get 18 months of work done in six months' time.

As this example illustrates, sometimes just putting people in a room together—even if it's too many people and even if it isn't exactly the right people—is enough to make significant progress. Here are a few steps you can take to get in the habit of making decisions "in the room":

Decide what you are going to decide

To make sure that the time people spend together is impactful, get out ahead of thinking through what decisions you're actually hoping to make in each synchronous meeting. Resist the urge to punt on these decisions and send things around for asynchronous feedback when the meeting is over, which often becomes a huge time-suck and, as Thomas Stubbs suggested, opens up lots of room for miscommunication and hurt feelings. If the group gets stuck trying to reach a "perfect" decision, try asking the question, "Would our current decision leave us in a better position than the one we are in right now?" If the answer is yes, commit to your decision in its current form, and commit to reevaluating that decision at an agreed-upon time in the future.

Practice time-boxing

One idea that informs multiple Agile practices is that of *time-boxing*, or establishing an absolute upper bound to the amount of time allotted for a given meeting. The first couple of times a team actually enforces a time box, it usually does not go that well. Critical decisions are left unmade, the most talkative people in the room go off on tangents, and everybody leaves feeling defeated and confused. But by the third or fourth time-boxed meeting, there is usually an appreciable change. Once people actually believe that a meeting will end within a given timeframe, they are much more inclined to prioritize the conversations that will help that meeting achieve its intended purpose. They are also much less likely to resist synchronous meetings out of fear that such meetings will go on forever and produce no tangible result.

Set expectations clearly

Regardless of whether you have a formalized agenda for a meeting, it is always helpful for people to know *why* you are asking for their time in the first place. Beyond being clear about the decisions you seek to make, it is helpful to tell the individual people you are inviting why their particular perspective is important and valuable to you. This makes it clear that you are actively looking for their input and collaboration rather than simply checking a box that corresponds to their role or team.

Don't call it a meeting!

For many modern organizations, "meeting" is nothing short of a dirty word. Though it might seem trivial, using a term like "hothouse" or "summit" can constitute an appreciable step toward helping people overcome the self-fulfilling belief that anything called a meeting will be a waste of time.

Disentangle "synchronous" from "colocated"

For remote and distributed teams, finding ways to work together "in the room" can be particularly challenging. But it is helpful to approach this challenge by clearly differentiating synchronous work from colocated work. Once this distinction has been made, it is much easier to ask questions like, "What kinds of decisions should we be making synchronously?" and, "How will we use asynchronous channels like email and document comments in a way that helps us achieve our goals?"

For teams of all kinds, drawing attention to the differences between synchronous and asynchronous modes of communication can open up space for more people to participate meaningfully in the process of making decisions, which in turn fosters a greater sense of shared accountability. Even though sending a PowerPoint deck around to 50 people and asking for feedback might feel like the easiest way to get something done, it is definitely not the most collaborative—or the most efficient.

Making Connections to "Scout and Scale"

Knowledge management can be a huge challenge for large and small organizations alike. As priorities shift and personnel turns over, there is a substantial risk of lessons that have already been learned going unheeded, and work that has already been done being redone. Embracing the guiding principle of collaborating early and often gives us one important step that we can take to reduce these risks: asking our colleagues what has already been done and by whom *before* we rush to executing new work within our particular team.

Embracing this approach allows us to take a broader view of our overall goals and shine a bigger and brighter light on the things that are already helping us to meet those goals. Shift7 CEO and former United States CTO Megan Smith described to me the *scout-and-scale* approach that she used successfully to address big, challenging problems in the public sector:

> In my work with the government and my work with Shift7, I have cultivated a scout-and-scale approach, which is to say, I don't build stuff, I find the people who are building it and connect them. The way to get to the future is solution making through inclusion, and the first step is often just asking, "What have you already got? Who already solved this problem?" It's usually multiple people, and we can connect these people to resources and to one another to scale these solutions. It's a systems-level intervention, very much in line with Agile principles.

Smith explained that her approach was inspired largely by venture capital firms, who she observed take two critical steps to catalyze their investments: "finding and supporting what works (or is promising)" early and often, and "networking their networks" to accelerate that positive momentum. In a blog post titled "Try this at Home: Scouting local solutions and scaling what's working (*http://bit.ly/2NkeiZ2*)" published by the Obama White House, Smith and her former White House colleagues Thomas Kalil and Aden van Noppen describe how Smith's scout-and-scale approach was used to address issues ranging from smart cities to police data access to Science, Technology, Engineering, and Mathematics (STEM) education:

Creative, committed, passionate people are solving challenges in their local communities. We can accelerate progress in more places by scouting to find these creative solutions or solutions-in-progress to tough problems that already exist. To scale, find, and share solutions with others working on the same challenges, use the Internet, and bring teams together.

Just as individual cities might have already made significant progress on a problem that is vexing a national government, individual teams often have first-hand knowledge of important business problems and opportunities that can be of great value to the organization at large. Connecting these teams with a scout-and-scale approach speaks directly to the value of visibility and collaboration between teams, and reinforces the idea that these teams are working together toward the same goals. It also provides organizational leaders with an opportunity to give credit and recognition to folks who might be outside of their immediate orbit.

Here are a few steps that every organization can take to implement a scout-and-scale approach to their work:

Get in the habit of asking what work has already been done and who is doing it.
In every organization, there is some degree of "tribal knowledge" that people share informally but is not captured in a permanent or easily retrievable way. One of the best ways to capture this knowledge is to dispel the assumption that if we haven't heard about something, it doesn't exist. Get in the habit of asking what's already been done and by whom. Questions like, "Have we tried this before?" or, "Who else in the organization is thinking about this same issue?" and even, "Are others outside our organization doing something relevant?" are great places to start.

Let your customer be the bridge between silos, products, or projects.
When scouting solutions from across the organization, don't forget who you're solving for. Keep customer goals and needs front and center, and you might discover unexpected opportunities to better serve your customers by making connections across functional or project-based teams. Ask teams and individuals to share the customer insights that led them to their particular solutions, and let those insights lead the way as you look for opportunities to connect and scale the work that has already been done.

Network your networks!

One powerful way to put scout-and-scale into practice is to provide your colleagues with multiple forums to share knowledge across teams. Drawing from the Spotify model, this might involve creating *guilds* in which people from across functions can share knowledge about common interests ranging from coffee to proprietary data analysis tools. Or, drawing from the Scrum framework, this might involve regular meetings in which "ambassadors" from each project team share their progress.

Have a shared language like "scout-and-scale" that speaks to the power of collaboration beyond squishy and easy-to-dismiss terms.

Simply saying, "We should all collaborate with each other more" is often not enough to drive action. As we discussed in Chapter 2, it is critical that you frame the idea of collaboration in language that your organization will understand and accept. Scout-and-scale provides a great template (and, if you are so inclined, some off-the-shelf language) for how you can use more specific and catchy language to generate interest in collaboration.

When we begin by asking what is already working, we give ourselves the opportunity to put more resources behind the solutions that are meeting the goals and needs of our customers. Adopting a scout-and-scale approach is one way that collaboration can break us out of the company-centric assumption that our first step should be to pitch a big project, secure a budget, or build something that will impress our colleagues and managers.

Agile Practice Deep Dive: The Daily Stand-Up

The daily stand-up, or daily scrum, is the first step that many teams take toward adopting Agile practices, and with good reason. This daily meeting provides a regularly scheduled opportunity for members of a team to align around their respective progress and their shared goals. And because it clocks in at under 15 minutes, the daily stand-up can usually be fitted into a team's existing schedule without feeling like an unreasonably large or disruptive ask.

The rules of the daily stand-up are fairly straightforward: every day, each member of the team stands up and shares information about the work they're doing as it relates to the team's goals. The entire meeting is to take no more than 15 minutes—a strict constraint that is reinforced by the fact that nobody is sitting down! Within the Scrum framework, each member of a team is tasked with answering these three specific questions:

- What did I do yesterday that helped the Development Team meet the Sprint Goal?
- What will I do today to help the Development Team meet the Sprint Goal?
- Do I see any impediment that prevents me or the Development Team from meeting the Sprint Goal?

For teams that are neither developing software nor working in sprints, these questions are often abstracted to the following:

- What did I do yesterday that helped the team meet its goals?
- What will I do today to help the team meet its goals?
- Do I see any impediments that prevent me or the team from meeting our goals?

Many teams abstract this even further, simply asking its members, "What did you do yesterday, what will you do today, and do you have any blockers?"

The daily stand-up can seem almost trivially simple, but it provides a hands-on introduction to some very powerful Agile ideas. First, it provides a relatively low-stakes way to introduce the practice of time-boxing. For many teams, it is unheard of for a 15-minute meeting to actually take 15 minutes. Once teams are accustomed to holding properly time-boxed daily stand-ups, they are often more comfortable applying the practice of time-boxing to longer meetings and meetings that involve people from outside of their immediate team.

Additionally, the daily stand-up introduces the idea of creating and protecting a regular cadence for communication. For many teams, synchronous team-wide meetings only occur when there is an immediate and transactional need for one. Holding space for your entire team to interact with one another every day, even if there is no proverbial fire to put out, helps create a true sense of shared purpose and accountability around both day-to-day tasks and broader team goals.

Of course, there are also plenty of ways for a daily stand-up meeting to go awry. In companies with a report-and-critique culture, the question of "What are you doing toward the team's goals" can feel like an accusation. One product manager I worked with described the daily stand-up as the "What have you done for the company lately" meeting, a rote and fruitless exercise in which team members defensively spit out as much as they possibly can about their own individual work without listening to or interacting with their colleagues.

Indeed, the simple fact of *holding* a daily stand-up will in no way guarantee that you are actually building a collaborative culture. As IBM CMO Michelle Peluso told me:

> *You can't check the box of "oh, we're doing stand-ups" and really under-stand what it means to be Agile. When you are truly practicing Agile, you're learning, starting to create your own things. It becomes reflexive. You keep going, you iterate, and you continue moving forward and living it. And once you get to that stage you never go back.*

In other words, the daily stand-up is at its most impactful and sustainable when your team feels a sense of collective ownership over this practice. Here are a few steps that you can take to make sure that your daily stand-up meetings are actually adding value and encouraging collaboration:

Be clear about why you are holding the stand-up

As with any Agile practice, the daily stand-up is only useful if you and your team have a clear understanding of *why* you're doing it in the first place. Take the time to discuss with your team what the purpose of this Agile practice might be, and be sure to tie it back to your guiding Agile principles and your organization or team's specific needs. For example, "We know that our organization is struggling to keep pace with our customers, and we have committed to the principle of collaborating early and often as a way to maximize the immediate impact of our customer research. *So,* we are going to have a daily stand-up meeting to stay focused on our customer-facing goals."

Treat the stand-up as a diagnostic

Because it is so simple and straightforward, the daily stand-up often becomes a powerful tool for diagnosing whether your team is stuck in report-and-critique mode or is building a truly collaborative culture. If people on your team roll their eyes or miss meetings, don't castigate them for not "doing Agile"—understand what isn't working for them and talk about how you can address this together. (As we discuss in Chapter 5, holding a retrospective is one way practice to group reflection on what is and is not working.)

Change the questions

The three canonical questions of the daily stand-up meeting were designed to keep teams tactically synchronized and focused on their overall goals. But the needs of every team are different, and nearly every Agile practitioner I know has at some point changed these questions to better reflect the needs of their team. Some have changed them to more explicitly encourage collaboration, like "What opportunities are there for your colleagues to help you today?" Some have gone so far as to ask much more personal questions like, "How much energy do you have today?" to address disconnects between team members' energy and capacity.

As we discussed in Chapter 2, making changes to any Agile practices, including the daily stand-up, should be done in the name of living up to your Agile principles and achieving your team or organization's specific goals. If you and your team are having trouble finding value in the daily stand-up, treat it as a learning opportunity rather than a procedural failure. Have a conversation with your team to find out what value people would like to get out of this practice and why they feel that they are not currently getting that value. Agree upon small changes you can make, one at a time, and reflect openly on whether they are helping you achieve your goals. Because the daily stand-up occurs every day, and because it is so often the first step that a team takes toward adopting Agile practices, it makes for a great opportunity to model a collaborative and principles-first approach to Agile in general.

Quick Wins to Put This Principle into Practice

Here are some steps that different teams can take to begin putting our Agile guiding principle of collaboration into practice:

For marketing teams, you might try...

...bringing together planners, agency partners, and creatives for regular synchronous meetings to guide campaigns from ideation through execution.

...responding to requests for asynchronous feedback ("Hey, can you take a quick look at the attached presentation?") by scheduling short timeboxed meetings to talk things through and make decisions.

For sales teams, you might try...

...sending a representative to product and marketing meetings to better understand the future of the product.

For executives, you might try...

...asking what has already been done toward addressing a given customer need or meeting a particular company goal before signing off on any new, big projects.

For product and engineering teams, you might try...

...inviting people from across the organization to attend a daily stand-up meeting so that they can learn more about this practice.

For an entire Agile organization, you might try...

...time-boxing meetings to facilitate decisive outcomes and minimize wasted time.

YOU MIGHT BE ON THE RIGHT TRACK IF:

People from different teams and functions are spending time together outside of formally scheduled, transactional meetings

As we have discussed throughout this chapter, actually following our guiding principle of collaboration is much more a question of culture than it is a question of org charts or calendar invites. A lot of important things can happen when people from across teams and functions are spending time together informally during meals, coffee breaks, and after-work activities. This does not mean that everybody should be, or should feel pressure to be, best friends. But the comfort and rapport that people develop through these informal interactions can have a tremendously positive effect on both an organization's culture and the quality of its work.

To keep the momentum going around this, you might want to:

- Make sure that organizational and team leaders are present during informal events like company lunches to avoid the implicit suggestion that people should be focused on "more important work."

- Utilize "Lunch Roulette" (*http://lunchroulette.us/*) or another mechanism for making informal connections across far-flung parts of your organization.

- Hold open "lunch-and-learn" meetings during which people can share interests outside of their day-to-day work (such as how to make great coffee at the office or how to research an awesome vacation).

Collaboration is taking place around upstream strategy as well as downstream tactics

In too many cases, "collaboration" happens only when the high-level strategic decisions for a project have already been made. For example, a broad group might be consulted on a specific wording choice for an advertising campaign or the specific shade of red to be used in an interface design, but the overall shape and objectives of the campaign or product are already set in stone. This is a classic symptom of an organization that is going through the motions of collaboration but still getting tied down by the Second Law of Organizational Gravity. When a broad and open conversation about a new idea is seen as an opportunity to make that idea better, not a threat to that idea's success or survival, an organization is well on its way to becoming more truly collaborative.

To keep the momentum going around this, you might want to:

- Hold open "demo days" during which teams can show off works in progress before they are finished and polished.

- Ask project leads to co-create a plan for how their respective projects will work together to meet customer needs and goals *before* any projects are approved or budgeted.

- Start each new project with a cross-functional work plan that explicitly includes inflection points for getting feedback from across the organization.

Nobody can really remember whose idea that was in the first place

When your organization has embraced the spirit and practice of collaboration, everybody feels invested in the ideas that are being developed and executed. Po.et CEO and former VP of Innovation at the *Washington Post* Jarrod Dicker pointed out to me that the most successful ideas are often the ones for which nobody can even remember whose idea it was in the first place. This creates a self-reinforcing loop of collaboration and success because the ideas that have been influenced, shaped, and reshaped by the broadest set of people and perspectives in the organizations are those receiving the most attention and resources. This is, in Dicker's words, a sure sign that an organization has transitioned from a "don't step on my toes" culture to a "please stomp all over my feet" culture.

To keep the momentum going around this, you might want to:

- Run ideas past individuals from across the organization when they are still in a relatively early form to incorporate diverse perspectives and create a shared sense of ownership.

- Recognize and incentivize collaborative efforts, and/or give employees ways to acknowledge and bring attention to one another's contributions.

- Conduct regular meetings during which people from different teams and functions can share works-in-progress, to incorporate perspectives and expertise from across the organization.

Anybody on your team can take a sick day without work grinding to a halt

One classic sign of a high-performing Agile team is that the team can continue to function in the absence of any of its individual members. This is not to say that multiple members of a team need to be experts in the same skill; I have worked with many Agile product teams, for example, that include only one engineer capable of writing a particular kind of code. But when a team is in the practice of collaborating early and often, the members of that team are able to regroup, adapt, and keep things moving forward. (Thanks to Andrew Stellman for this suggestion!)

To keep the momentum going around this, you might want to:

- Hold a daily stand-up meeting at the beginning of each day, giving your team the opportunity to regroup and adapt as needed.

- Provide opportunities for members of your team to share their skills and knowledge with one another. This could involve pairing team members with different skills to work on the same thing, or hosting informal gatherings during which team members can share their skills with the group at large.

- "Trade" a member of your team with a member of another team for a day or a week to expand your team's skills and knowledge beyond its immediate boundaries.

YOU MIGHT BE GOING ASTRAY IF:

Your meetings feel like elementary school book reports

For organizations that have not evolved past a report-and-critique culture, meetings can feel more like elementary school book reports than opportunities to collaboratively make important decisions. If your meetings involve taking turns spouting off the most defensible thing you can conjure while everybody else dozes off or dreads their turn in front of the room, you've got some work to do.

If this is happening, you might want to:

- Acknowledge that the way you are currently holding meetings is not working and ask for the help and support of your colleagues in making your meetings better. Sometimes, just opening up this conversation is enough to begin steering things in the right direction and create a shared sense of accountability around meetings instead of treating them like something that is being forced on everybody.

- Impose strict time limits on your meetings, and enforce them ruthlessly. When people realize that their time is truly limited, they are more likely to make the most of it. Note that it generally takes at least three to four meetings for people to get used to this and actually begin managing their time differently.

- Try making your meetings optional and see who shows up. This will help you to understand who is currently getting value from a given meeting. Work with those people to understand why they find the meeting valuable and what you can do collectively to extend that value to others.

Everything shared between teams is finished and polished

Everybody wants to do a good job, and presenting something that is finished, polished, and impressive often feels like a surefire way to boost your status in an organization. But finished and polished things often send the wrong message: "I want you to be impressed by this, but I don't really want you to participate." Even worse, when feedback is given on something that is polished and finished, it is often met with heavy sighs and huffs of, "Well, this is already pretty much finished," or, "My boss already signed off on this, I can't really change anything."

If this is happening, you might want to:

- Have a "no PowerPoints" rule when new ideas and initiatives are being discussed, an idea popularized by Jeff Bezos at Amazon (*http://bit.ly/2BWFM4I*). The time that goes into finishing and polishing a PowerPoint presentation often has nothing to do with the quality of the ideas being presented, and it certainly offers no value to the customer or end user.

- Conduct short, high-energy structured brainstorming sessions with people from multiple teams and functions to think about how a particular customer need or goal might be addressed. The tools and practices commonly associated with Design Thinking can be particularly valuable here.

- Put new ideas and works-in-progress in a public and highly visible space to invite serendipitous feedback from anybody who happens to be present.

Your inbox is full of requests for asynchronous feedback

Talking through works-in-progress synchronously can be awkward, uncomfortable, and challenging. It is much easier to simply send an email and say, "Please send me your feedback." Your bases are covered in that you *technically* asked for feedback, and you can add as many people as you want to the distribution with minimal additional time expenditure on your part. But for each person you chose to copy in the thread, there is now a new task on their desk that they must process, prioritize, and find time to address.

If this is happening, you might want to:

- Be clear about *who* you will ask for feedback, and *why*. You can use a formalized framework such as a RACI (Responsible, Accountable, Consulted, Informed) Matrix, or just keep an informal list and make sure each person on that list knows what you expect from them and why.

- Reply to requests for asynchronous feedback with an offer to meet up for 10 minutes and provide your feedback in person. If the person who emailed you doesn't have the time to spare, they likely were not all that interested in your feedback in the first place.

- Get in the habit of including the kind of feedback you need and the time-frame in which you need it in your email subject lines. For example, "Newest Version of Campaign Plan [Approval Needed by Friday]," or, "Latest Product Mockups [FYI, No Feedback Needed]."

Summary: Building a Culture of Collaboration

For people whose calendars are already packed with tedious and seemingly unnecessary meetings, the idea of *more* collaboration can seem wasteful and counterproductive. But truly building a culture of collaboration is about much more than sitting in a room while somebody tells you about the work they just finished. Making the choice to err on the side of openness—to share things *before* they are finished and polished, and to ask for input while that input can still inform a project's overall shape and direction—can contribute to a truly collaborative culture. When we work toward developing such a culture, the value we deliver to our customers is not bounded by the gaps and silos in our org chart.

5

Agile Means That We Plan for Uncertainty

It is more or less a given at this point that the world is changing quickly and organizations must become more flexible. But actually creating and protecting space to act on that need for flexibility is a huge challenge, and one for which Agile principles and practices are particularly well suited. Agile not only acknowledges the reality of an uncertain and fast-changing world, but also provides an actual structure for navigating that uncertainty.

Following the guiding principle of planning for uncertainty provides organizations with a way to balance short-term flexibility with long-term planning. The Agile Manifesto reminds us to value "responding to change over following a plan," and Agile gives us a way to formally build responding to change into the actual plans that we follow. Here, again, Agile practices give us concrete steps we can take to become more flexible and responsive, while Agile principles give us a directional sense of how those practices can change our work for the better.

Many organizations already have initiatives under way to become more adaptable, presenting a great opportunity to integrate your Agile principles with existing organizational language and ideas. One organization we worked with, for example, used the lens of "external focus" to describe how they would keep pace with the fast-changing world around them. If your organization is already undergoing some kind of "innovation" work, this might be a great way to add structure and specificity to the lofty goals that often accompany such initiatives.

Escaping the Third Law of Organizational Gravity

Flexibility is one of the most obvious and well-understood reasons why organizations are drawn to Agile in the first place. However, most organizations still struggle to actually change course in substantial ways, even when numerous people within an organization—including senior leaders—agree that adaptability is critical for that organization's success.

The reason for this can largely be attributed to what I call the *Third Law of Organizational Gravity*: a project in motion will stay in motion unless acted upon by the senior-most person who approved it (Figure 5-1). In other words, if a particular project, initiative, or product idea has the sign-off of a VP or C-level executive, it is likely to continue apace even if it is clearly not going to meet the desired customer need or company goal. After all, what's the point of bringing bad news to your superiors when *they* will likely be held accountable for a project's perhaps-inevitable failure?

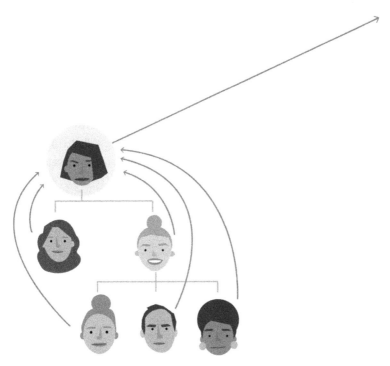

Figure 5-1. The Third Law of Organizational Gravity: A project in motion will stay in motion unless acted upon by the senior-most person who approved it. Note all the lines of attention focused squarely on the highest point of the org chart.

Returning to our First Law of Organizational Gravity, the senior leaders who would need to intervene are often the farthest removed from direct interaction with customers. This creates a self-perpetuating system in which it is all but impossible for organizations to adjust course based on new learnings from their customers. By the time senior leaders get the feedback that should result in a course change, it has usually been scrubbed and sanitized to the point where it reads more like, "Great job, boss!"

This dynamic explains why people in organizations often continue to work on projects that they know are not going to succeed. It also helps to explain why embarrassingly bad marketing campaigns and #socialmediafails persist in this era of rapid customer feedback. In the calculus of organizational politics, public embarrassment can often seem less risky than telling your boss that something they signed off on is a bad idea.

Personal courage is certainly one way that individuals can work against this law of organizational gravity—but it is not enough. The only way to ensure that change will happen is to make change *part of your process*. In other words, those executives signing off on projects need to understand that making room for change is an inextricable part of the projects themselves. In doing so, adjusting course feels more like a commendable example of foresight, and less like a regrettable instance of failure.

Kathryn Kuhn, an experienced Agile practitioner and advocate who has worked with organizations like Teradata, Oracle, and Hewlett-Packard, described to me how a large financial services organization was able to better plan for uncertainty by adding shorter, quarterly cycles to their existing years-long planning cycles, and framing up this shorter cadence in a language that resonated with the organization itself:

> We can't always get an organization to stop doing years-long planning cycles. But we can get them to add a quarterly business review. It's pretty simple—you start reflecting on how you did last quarter; then you bring in additional information that you want people to know. Maybe there's a new Gartner study about how the market is changing, new regulatory requirements, new initiatives from company leaders, or new information about our customers. Bring that information into the room, describe what you've learned since the last time you discussed your plans, and then look ahead. Can you look at some of your initiatives and, based on what you now know, declare them "done enough"? If you're 85% of the way toward achieving your goal with one initiative, can you strategically shift your resources to another initiative where you're only 20% done?

> With this approach, we were able to get the whole bank on a cadence of quarterly planning events. It gave them a way to address all kinds of things, like running through audits with thousands of remediations that would have previously ground the bank to a halt. Instead, they were able to pull the work apart in these quarterly planning events, realize what they could and could not get done, and knock off the highest-priority items. We could have a conversation about which features were customer-delighters, and what the scope of these features might be. We could discuss the trade-offs of each approach, rather than letting them get decided by inertia and inaction.

> One key to our success was using the language of the organization itself—terms like "good enough for now," and "done enough." Or, "great idea, not

yet." This gave people a vocabulary to talk about prioritization without being too technical or too dismissive.

As this example illustrates, even in organizations that plan in year-long cycles, there is room to build in more frequent opportunities to share knowledge and adjust course. And, as we discussed in Chapter 2, incorporating language that is already well understood within an organization can help make new ideas and practices feel more approachable and applicable, even as they pose a substantial challenge to business as usual.

The Paradox of Agile: Using Structure to Achieve Flexibility

At the heart of most Agile methodologies is the somewhat paradoxical idea that a regular cadence creates *more* room for flexibility. This is because a fixed and finite cadence—like the Agile sprints we discussed in Chapter 3—makes responding to change a regular part of the way we work, not a challenge to the way we work.

When I began learning about Agile, I was concerned that a more fixed and frequent structure would make my team slower and less responsive. Committing to getting something done every two weeks felt much more rigid and regimented than planning to get something done roughly every couple of months or, even better, "whenever it's good enough." To my surprise and delight, though, a shorter fixed cadence actually resulted in my team making bolder and more exciting choices. We were able to build and test lightweight prototypes for new product directions, knowing that we could always abandon those directions if we learned that they were not adding value for our customers. And we were able to better plan around the quarterly and yearly goals of the organization knowing that we had the power to adjust course every couple weeks if we did not appear to be hitting those goals.

Sure enough, nearly all organizations operate under plans that extend beyond the two-week increments of a standard Agile sprint, whether it is a quarterly product roadmap at a small technology startup or a yearly budget for a large enterprise. Agile practitioners (especially newly indoctrinated ones who have been through a lot of training) often see any long-term cadence as a threat to true agility, and eventually declare that being truly Agile is "just not possible in an organization this large and bureaucratic." Alan Bunce, a consultant and former marketing leader at organizations like IBM and Salesforce.com, described to me how the most successful Agile practitioners seek out a balance between long-term planning and short-term adjustment:

> *I've never worked at a place, no matter how "Agile," where you didn't start the year by thinking about what your budget's going to be. Especially if you're working at companies that are gearing up to go public, it's not like you can say "Oh, we don't know how much we're going to spend—we're Agile!" The way budgeting cycles are done, sales teams and executives think about what they think they can hit or what their targets ought to be for the year. Then, marketing's budget is backed out from that.*
>
> *Agile often carries this sense of, "Hey, at any moment we can do anything"—the reality is you can't! You have a budget. And very quickly that budget starts to get carved up. That still leaves a lot of room for agility, but it's by no means a blank sheet of paper. You need to strike a balance between long-term and off-the-cuff.*
>
> *What that balance looks like will depend a lot on how an organization uses those long-term cycles. Are they chiseled in stone, or are they more guidelines, with an understanding there will be some adjustment? If those longer-term guidelines are used not as the absolute truth, but as a directional guide, that still leaves a lot of room for agility. But once things become fixed and bureaucratic, "you said $10.1 million, not $9.9 million," then things get trickier.*

As both this example and Kathryn Kuhn's story from earlier in this chapter illustrate, having yearly plans in place does not mean that we must abandon our quest for agility. If anything, it means that we must be even more proactive and disciplined about establishing shorter cadences that we can use to keep our team's work aligned with those longer-term plans—and to incorporate the new things we learn from our customers along the way.

Here are a few steps you can take to keep your team's short-term cadences aligned with long-term goals and planning structures:

List out the fixed cadences of your organization and work with, not against, them

Does your organization have a yearly budgeting cycle? A two-year strategic planning cycle? A quarterly goal-setting process? Draw them all out on a sheet of paper and write down what is actually decided upon in each cycle, who is making those decisions, and what they expect as a result. Then, think about how you can build a shorter cadence around these cycles that creates more room for flexibility while respecting and accommodating organizational planning cycles that are unlikely to change.

Celebrate change

When we are planning only in long-term cycles, change of any kind can seem like a demand for frustrating rework. Adding shorter-term cycles allows us more time to get out ahead of changes to our initial plan and reconcile new information with our longer-term goals. We can draw attention to this newfound flexibility by celebrating change rather than decrying it. In other words, if we realize two short cycles into a much longer cycle that we have been on the wrong track, rather than saying, "Crap, there goes four weeks of work down the drain," we can say, "We are so lucky that we caught this now and we can adjust course while there's still time for us to hit our quarterly goals."

Focus on what's possible

The tension between short-term agility and long-term planning is one that never fully goes away, and inevitably creates situations in which your team cannot do the exact thing it wants to do at the exact time it wants to do so. But blaming the organization at large for not being as "Agile" as it should be is likely only to hurt your team's morale and motivation. Instead, focus on what *can* be done given the real-world constraints of your organization.

In many cases, embracing this do-what's-possible approach can actually help make long-term planning cycles more useful by clarifying their purpose and the expectations they create. As teams and organizations work toward finding the right balance of short-term and long-term planning, they are better equipped to understand and appreciate the value that both can offer.

The Double-Edged Sword of Experimentation

Inevitably, planning for uncertainty means making our best guess and moving forward *before* we know that everything we do will be a success. In many Agile and Agile-adjacent approaches, particularly the Lean Startup world, "experimentation" is often framed as the best way for teams and organizations to validate new product ideas and directions in a fast-changing world.

Real-life organizations, unfortunately, do not provide the pristine and sterile environs of a well-maintained laboratory. The idea of experimentation is an important one to bring to an organization, but it can also be a dangerous one if it imparts a sense of scientific certainty that ultimately contradicts the messy and fast-changing nature of the real world. At its best, experimentation can help us understand the uncertainty out there in the world, but it can never eliminate that uncertainty.

For teams and individuals looking to make definitively correct decisions, this can be a tough pill to swallow. And, sure enough, there are certain types of decisions that are easier to definitively prove out with an experiment than others. Deciding, for example, whether to make the "Home" button on a web page round or square would not be a particularly difficult thing to prove out via quantitative A/B testing. But suppose that you need to decide whether an entirely new line of business is worth getting into or whether an existing product will sink or swim when introduced to an entirely new market. While it is certainly possible—and worthwhile—to design an experiment that would help you answer these questions (the book *The Lean Startup* (*http://bit.ly/2pIwpym*) is full of great examples), no such experiment would give you the same sense of irrefutable and scientific certainty as that simple A/B test.

In theory, this should mean that teams and organizations wind up spending more time on the more difficult and ambiguous experiments that validate complex, market-based decisions. But in practice, it often means the opposite: teams and organizations wind up spending a disproportionate amount of time on the experiments that are easiest to validate in absolute quantitative terms, even if these are the least impactful for the business.

When my business partners and I are working with organizations, we often ask them to map out the experiments they are running on a quadrile we call *Integrated Data Thinking*, as shown in Figure 5-2. This quadrile maps out data-related initiatives along an axis from "discovery" to "optimization" and "qualitative" to "quantitative." My Sudden Compass business partner Tricia Wang developed this framework after working with many organizations that had been inadvertently over-relying upon quantitative, optimization-level work such as A/B testing while neglecting the much more difficult and ambiguous work of validating discovery-level decisions and running experiments that are primarily proven out via qualitative data.

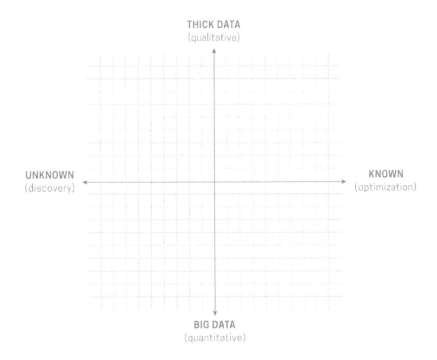

Figure 5-2. Sudden Compass's Integrated Data Thinking model.

Nearly every company with which we have run this exercise winds up with a completed quadrile that leans very heavily toward quantitative optimization at the lower right. But when we ask those same organizations to map the business questions that are keeping them awake at night along the x-axis from discovery to optimization, the quadrile leans just as heavily toward discovery on the left. It is not uncommon, for example, for an organization to be most preoccupied with major discovery-level questions like "How can we grow our business into new markets" while running the vast majority of its experiments around incremental optimizations to existing products, markets, or messages. Simply acknowledging this disconnect is often enough for individuals to take notice and start exploring new ways to run qualitative and discovery-level experiments in the upper-left quadrile.

Unsurprisingly, one great example of such an experiment comes directly from the Lean Startup world. Former Lean Startup Productions CEO and cofounder Sarah Milstein described to me how she was able to run simple, low-cost experiments to validate new product ideas, and how qualitative data often factored into these experiments:

> When we were launching a new conference as part of Lean Startup Productions, we had the idea that we should sell tickets for a remote version. We didn't think it would be terribly popular, so we hypothesized that we would sell about 10 tickets. And the day we put it up for sale, we sold 100 tickets. This was a really big sign for us that our thinking wasn't caught up to where our customers were. And if we didn't have a hypothesis, 10 and 100 would have looked the same. This kind of hypothesis-driven experiment is just as valuable if it turns out you're wrong—you're not even aiming for rightness necessarily, you're aiming to gauge where your current thinking is in relation to the actual customer you are serving.

> It's also worth noting that people can get fetishistic about experimentation pretty easily, to the detriment of its purpose. Sometimes, an experiment can be much more about qualitative signals; for example, the way people start using a phrase that's in your marketing materials. This approach is officially called "artifact analysis." If we change the wording on our website to "inquiries," for example, will the content of the emails we receive start to be different? We don't always have a number, but we know what we're looking for and why we're looking.

As this story illustrates, the easiest things to test and measure are not always the most important things to test and measure. When we begin by asking the questions that are most important to our business and our customers, not the questions that seem easiest to answer with a quantitative experiment, we are being true to the complexity and uncertainty of the world around us.

Agile Is Uncertain, Too

Perhaps the most common antipattern I've seen in organizations seeking to implement Agile practices goes a little something like this: "We understand that the world changes quickly, so we are going to implement a set of Agile practices...*that are guaranteed to work forever and that we will never need to change.*" Planning for uncertainty in our organizations also means planning for uncertainty in the way we approach Agile—which can be very challenging for organizations that see Agile as a box they can check off rather than an ongoing journey that will itself require a constant embrace of change.

To navigate this change, teams and organizations must take shared owner-ship of the processes they use, and build enough trust and transparency to speak candidly about what is working for them, what is not working for them, and why. This is often difficult to accomplish when Agile is seen as simply a mandate that comes down from on high or is brought in by an army of external consultants. Even when a team of well-intentioned practitioners is driving the adoption of their own Agile practices, taking time to reflect on and refine those practices can prove challenging. Abhishek Gupta, an engineering manager who has worked with companies like Apple and American Express, described to me how opening a conversation about the goals of a team's Agile practices can lead to difficult but important changes to that team's routines and rituals:

One big challenge with Agile is that it becomes a set of things you need to do, without an understanding of the "why." This is made even worse when Agile is treated as a silver bullet. "Our projects will be great, because we're doing Agile!" That doesn't translate if the spirit isn't there. For people who deeply care about product quality, Agile is a means, not an end. To con-fuse the process and the outcome is at the core of the problem here. If you don't care about product quality, if you don't care about delivering value to your customers, then Agile won't save you.

I worked with one team that had been "doing Agile" for a while when I started working with them. I asked them, "Is this something you see as valuable?" And the initial responses I got were, "Oh yes, very, very valua-ble." So for two months, I attended their Agile meetings to see what was working well for them. Every meeting was a similar thing; show off your tickets in [software development tool] Jira, say what are you working on, is it done, is it not done. The team was much more focused on closing actual tickets than they were on understanding the impact of the work they were doing; it was a lot of process management without giving much thought to actual outcomes. In other words, it was a lot of busywork.

So, after a few months, I had to say to the team, "How is this actually use-ful to you?" I had a lot of one-on-one meetings with engineers asking for this kind of candid feedback. And what I heard was that they found it use-ful to not have to work on too many things at once, to be able to know what they were working on, and have that kind of focus. So we talked about how we could retain that focus, but bring in more big-picture, direc-tional thinking to make sure that focus was understood through the value we were creating for our customers. This meant stepping away from a lot of by-the-book Agile rituals, and asking as a team, "How can we work in a way that best achieves the outcomes we want for ourselves and our customers?"

Indeed, truly embracing the Agile principle of planning for uncertainty means that we must regularly ask our teams that very question, and be open to our answer changing as our goals, our teams, and our customers change. In most cases, this eventually involves giving up the sense of comfort and safety that comes from doing Agile "by the book" and finding the particular set of practices that works best for the individuals on our team. This can be a scary step, but it is worth remembering that the set of practices and frameworks that we now call Agile were themselves developed through trial and error by practitioners before the word "Agile" was ever used to describe them. When we understand our organizational needs and we follow our guiding principles, we open ourselves up to discovering new ways of working, and we empower our teams to feel ownership over them.

Agile Practice Deep Dive: The Retrospective

If Agile is the engine that helps you achieve escape velocity and overcome the laws of organizational gravity, the *retrospective* is the valve that stops that engine from overheating and burning out. A retrospective is a meeting at the end of a sprint or the completion of a project during which a team reflects on the way they work together and identifies changes they can make for the next sprint or project. Note that the goal of a retrospective is explicitly not to critique the actual work that was just completed, but rather to reflect on how the team completed that work.

The retrospective constitutes an important opportunity for teams to build a shared sense of purpose and ownership around the way they work. It is a chance to first ask the question, "Is the way we're working helping us live up to our principles and achieve our goals," and then, "What are we going to do about it next time?"

For many teams I've worked with, especially those outside of product and engineering, speaking openly about what is and is not working can be an uncomfortable prospect. People often assume that the way they currently work must have been put into place for a very good reason, and that questioning it might amount to undermining somebody else's experience or authority. But I have been truly amazed at how many times a particular practice or artifact—like a regularly scheduled meeting that provides no real value or a campaign planning template that demands way too much information—turns out to be a simple historical accident that nobody has felt empowered to reevaluate. I have participated in many retrospectives, for example, in which somebody sheepishly suggests that a long-standing practice is no longer serving the team, only for everybody else in the room—including that team's leader—to react in swift and violent agreement. Moments like this can have an immediate and incredibly positive effect on a team's morale and productivity, but they simply do not occur unless you create space for them.

One of the fantastic things about retrospectives is that you can run them at the end of any project, regardless of whether that project involves any other Agile practices. Adding a retrospective to any regularly scheduled work such as a monthly newsletter or quarterly planning meeting can open up a new kind of space for teams to discuss how they work together and why. Emma Obanye, founder of Mindful Team, explained to me how she came to value the retrospective as one of the most important tools for building trust and communication on a team:

> Most issues can be solved with communication, and a lot of companies miss the human side of things. They think that Agile is going to make people faster, but people are not robots! And there are a lot of silly issues and miscommunications that can become big problems unless you bring people together for an open dialogue. Sometimes, just the safety net of being able to express yourself in front of your team is enough to get started— and once you have that, you start to get a team into the state of flow. And for me, that starts with the retrospective. Each Agile ceremony has its reason. But to me, the retrospective is the key to continuous improvement. Without that, a strict and regimented framework is all you've got.

> We've talked to a lot of Scrum masters who have trouble communicating the value of Agile to their teams. And if you have that problem, you need to start from the beginning. You need to open up that dialogue, and give everybody on the team the opportunity to say what they really feel. There will almost certainly be conflict, but that conflict is good—it's what drives you to the next level. Without bringing that conflict into the open, a lot of teams are stuck in that first level, unable to work through the very first challenges that they find in an newly formed team.

Retrospectives are often challenging for the very reason that they are ulti-mately so valuable: they open up a space where people can voice their doubts, questions, and uncertainties about the way that they work together. These con-versations are rarely comfortable, and they rarely yield easy or certain answers. But the simple fact of the retrospective is often enough to begin addressing the unspoken beliefs and assumptions that can leave teams feeling stuck and disem-powered. Here are a few tips for keeping your retrospective on track:

Model vulnerability and uncertainty

If you are the person bringing Agile practices to your team, your team-mates look to you to understand how they are "supposed" to behave during a retrospective. This might leave you feeling like you need to have all the right answers, or to defend the Agile practices you've introduced. But the best thing you can do for your team is to model the kind of openness and honesty that will enable you to continuously adapt and improve. If some-body asks about a particular practice and you don't have a good answer, feel free to say, "I don't really know. What does everybody else think?"

Stay focused on what you are going to do next time

In many organizations, taking time to reflect on the way a team works only happens when there is a major problem. As a result, retrospectives can devolve into evasiveness and finger-pointing. The engineering teams at Etsy solved this problem by holding what they call "blameless postmortems (*http://bit.ly/2QwFvd2*)," in which participants can openly reflect on mis-takes they made without fearing retribution. But another step you can take to avoid the blame game is to shift the conversation toward what you will do differently for the next sprint or project. For example, "Regardless of who was responsible for what happened last time, what can we all do together next time to make things better?"

Treat future changes as experiments, not mandates

Regularly scheduled retrospectives provide your team with the opportunity to adjust course after each sprint or project. This means that there is very little risk associated with trying a new practice or approach; after all, if it isn't working, you will have the opportunity to change it or roll it back dur-ing your next retrospective. Remind your team that every change you make is essentially an experiment; you won't know whether it works until you try it, and you are prepared to adjust course based on what you learn.

Keep your principles in focus

I've often found it helpful to have my team or organization's guiding Agile principles physically present during a retrospective. This helps to keep the team focused not just on *how* they are working together, but also on *why* they are changing the way they work in the first place. These principles can also serve as a powerful mediator when there is a disagreement, enabling you to ask, "Which of these approaches is most aligned with our guiding principles?" rather than, "Which of these approaches do we like more?"

Hold space for what is working

Although running a retrospective is a critical way to adjust course when things are not working well for your team, it is also a critical way to acknowledge the things that *are* working well for your team. One approach I've found helpful is to ask each team member to quickly write down three things that worked well and three things they think could be changed for the next sprint or project. This gives equal time to the things that are worth protecting and the things that stand to be refined.

Break the ice

A team's first couple of retrospectives can be particularly awkward. Sometimes, it is helpful to bring a sense of fun and ease to a retrospective by starting with an icebreaker, or framing the retrospective itself as a kind of game. Mindful Team, whose cofounder Emma Obanye provided the insightful commentary about retrospectives earlier in this chapter, offers a card game called The Retrospective Game (*http://bit.ly/2yde68f*) that can provide a great first step for teams that are not used to sharing reflections in a group.

Finally, and perhaps most importantly, resist the temptation to cancel your retrospectives if you have a lot of work to do. For teams and organizations that see Agile just as a means to increase velocity, the retrospective can seem like a waste of productive time—after all, you aren't actually making anything, just sitting around and talking about how you make things. But making time for a team to reflect on how it works is a non-negotiable if you want that team to embrace any new ways of working. In the absence of a retrospective it is inevitable that any set of Agile practices will fail to achieve their full potential, as the team implementing those practices comes to see them as just another form of "business as usual" that they are powerless to question or adapt.

Quick Wins to Put This Principle into Practice

Here are some steps that different teams can take to begin putting our Agile guiding principle of planning for uncertainty into practice:

For marketing teams, you could try...

...setting a regular cadence to reevaluate big-picture questions, such as "What is our brand promise?" and "What is our brand voice?"

...providing real-time feedback on the performance of active campaigns during daily or weekly meetings. (Thanks to Andrea Fryrear for this suggestion!)

For sales teams, you could try...

...assembling small "SWAT teams" of salespeople designed to test new products and markets. (Thanks to Alan Bunce for this suggestion!)

...running a retrospective after an important pitch or sales call.

For executives, you could try...

...communicating clearly what is set in stone and what is subject to flexibility during long-term planning cycles.

For product and engineering teams, you could try...

...setting aside one sprint to prototype what your product would look like if you had the opportunity to reinvent it from scratch.

For an entire Agile organization, you could try...

...creating temporary, cross-functional tasks forces to run shared retrospectives on projects that involve work from multiple teams.

...explicitly including opportunities to reevaluate the overall course of a project within every new project plan.

YOU MIGHT BE ON THE RIGHT TRACK IF:

You and your team feel a little bit uncertain and out of your depth most of the time

Planning for uncertainty means accepting uncertainty. Truly embracing this guiding principle means giving up the posture of certainty that often wins arguments, settles debates, and stops organizations from seeking out and responding to mission-critical new information. Rather than suppressing or resisting your uncertainty and discomfort, let them guide you to constantly learn more about your customers and the fast-changing world that you share with them.

To keep the momentum going around this, you might want to:

- Hold regular "inspiration sessions" to share new information about your customers and your market with people from across the organization.

- Bring open-ended questions about your customers to other parts of the organization, without having a clear sense of what you think the answer should or might be.

- Get into the habit of presenting multiple solutions to a given problem, opening up space to acknowledge both the benefits and the limitations of each approach rather than presenting a single "correct" approach.

You are regularly killing off projects that are not creating value for your customers

In most organizations, abandoning or killing off a project feels like failure. The person responsible for that project runs the risk of losing status, resources, and in some cases even their job. But, in organizations that have truly embraced uncertainty, killing off a project is a sign of success. It means that you are open to the possibility of your customers and your market changing, and will not sink additional resources into something that you have learned is no longer likely to succeed. If you've reached the point where a project lead is comfortable saying, "I think we should kill this idea and put our resources elsewhere," you are well on your way to building a truly Agile organization.

To keep the momentum going around this, you might want to:

- Acknowledge and celebrate team and project leads who are brave enough to adjust course and substantially redirect a project already in progress.

- Make sure that the success of every project is measured not just by operational metrics such as "on time" and "on budget," but also by the value it creates for your customers.

- Keep a record of what projects were abandoned and for what reason so as to avoid these projects being accidentally revisited without this context.

When specific Agile practices are not working for your team, you work together to change them

It might feel like the ultimate end goal of an Agile journey is to have your entire organization 100% onboarded to a single, stable, and consistent set of practices and rituals. But this goal runs deeply counter to the very first statement of the Agile Manifesto: "Individuals and interactions over processes and tools." As the individuals in your organization and the individuals you serve change, so too must your Agile practices. If the way you work is evolving to meet the needs of your team, this is a sign that you are being true to the principles of Agile, not a sign that you have failed at implementing the practices of Agile.

To keep the momentum going around this, you might want to:

- Share information about your evolving Agile practices beyond your team. Some teams I've worked with, for example, send out memos stating what change they made, what effect they hoped this change would have, what effect it *actually* had, and what they are going to do about it moving forward.

- Have open and candid conversations with your team, at both a group and one-on-one level, about what value they are deriving from Agile practices.

- Put a name to the set of practices that is working for you and your team, such as the Spotify model or Enterprise Design Thinking, to foster a sense of collective ownership of the practices that you are utilizing.

YOU MIGHT BE GOING ASTRAY IF:

Your organization demands 100% certainty before committing to a decision

When I coach organizations through the practice of experimentation, the question I am asked most often is, "When can we be 100% sure that we're right?" This is often the question people are being asked by their managers, and it is a much more dangerous question that it seems. When organizations demand 100% certainty, they implicitly encourage the suppression or omission of any new information that complicates their existing plans. Thus, the organizations that demand the most certainty actually leave themselves most vulnerable to the unknown and unexpected.

If this is happening, you might want to:

- Initiate a conversation about the unseen risk we incur when we strive for absolute certainty in an uncertain world.

- Formally make "questions we can't answer" or "things that might change" a part of your project plans, to communicate that uncertainty is inevitable and prepare for alternate outcomes.

- Map out decisions you're making on a matrix from low impact to high impact, and low certainty to high certainty. This can help you to differentiate "sure things" from important things and enable a more informed conversation about risk.

You are withholding important information until the next yearly planning or budgeting meeting

One of the dangers with regular organizational cadences is that they can compel people to *withhold* important information until what they consider to be the officially sanctioned time and place. This can happen when engineers don't share critical blockers until the next daily stand-up, or when marketers shelve customer insights until the next campaign planning cycle. This self-imposed delay can result in wasted resources, missed opportunities, and crippling bottlenecks when that regular cadence does come around.

If this is happening, you might want to:

- Schedule more frequent "check-ins" between infrequent meetings to track progress and share new information.

- Have a discussion with your team about what type of information constitutes an out-of-cadence "emergency" and should be communicated immediately, and to whom it should be communicated.

- Create a formal template or practice for handling "emergency" information that comes in from customers, clients, or executives. This helps you retain some sense of structure and procedure while still accounting for the reality that important new information could arise at any time.

You are working a certain way "because it's Agile"—and that's it

Just because a particular practice is Agile does not mean that it's a good fit for your organization or that it will help you deliver more value to your customers in a faster and more flexible way. If the best justification you can think of for working a certain way is "because it's Agile," then it is very unlikely that you and your teammates are cultivating a shared sense of purpose and ownership over the way that you work together.

If this is happening, you might want to:

- Communicate clearly that whatever practices you implemented initially are only a starting point. Set clear expectations that the way your team or organization is working six months from now *should* and *must* be different from what that framework or methodology looks like on paper.

- Push back on absolute quantitative metrics for Agile adoption (such as "20% of our projects must be Agile within the next five years") because they can easily turn the entire universe of Agile practices and principles into a meaningless checkbox.

- Run a deprivation test; cease all Agile rituals and ceremonies for a week, and see what happens. Afterward, run a retrospective with your team and use this as an opportunity to "hit reset" and initiate a frank conversation about what is and is not working.

Summary: Change Is Good, If You Want It

In the wise words of psychologist Virginia Satir, "Most people prefer the certainty of misery to the misery of uncertainty." Agile gives us a way to make uncertainty appreciably less miserable by giving ourselves consistent and predictable opportunities to incorporate new information from an inconsistent and unpredictable world. When we embrace the idea that more structure can ultimately offer us more flexibility, we can use the day-to-day practices of our team as a tangible lever to reduce our fear of change and the missed opportunities that come with it. Planning for uncertainty turns fear that new information will derail our progress into gratitude that new information can be incorporated into our work before it is too late.

6

Agile Means That We Follow All Three of These Guiding Principles to Be Fast, Flexible, and Customer-First

The three guiding principles we have covered so far capture three concepts that are at the very heart of what makes Agile such a powerful movement: customer centricity, collaboration, and openness to change. Committing to any one of these three guiding principles can make an immediate difference for any team or organization looking to work with, not against, the realities of a fast-changing world. But the real magic happens when these three principles are applied together to create a harmonious cycle of learning, collaborating, and delivering.

As this cycle gains momentum, so too does the belief that real change is possible. The alchemical union of principles and practices at the heart of Agile provides teams not just with a new way of working, but with the permission to ask *why* they are working a certain way—often for the first time. As teams take more ownership over the way that they work, they become more comfortable challenging the fundamental beliefs and expectations that have allowed "business as usual" to persist through prior attempts at organizational change.

Creating space for meaningful, sustainable, and ongoing change means accepting the fact that there is no single framework or set of practices that will lead every organization to guaranteed success. Agile reminds us that organizations are not operational puzzles to be solved, but rather collections of individuals working together to meet the fast-changing needs of their customers. This means that every individual has a role to play in making their organization fast, flexible, and customer-first. In this sense, "Agile for Everybody" is not just a statement about the broad applicability of Agile principles, but also a reminder that Agile is at its most potent and transformative when *everybody* in an organization, regardless of their level, their team, or their role, applies those principles to their day-to-day work.

Leadership in the Agile Organization

Many of my conversations with Agile practitioners took a swift and immediate turn toward the topic of leadership. A 2006 *Harvard Business Review* article titled "Embracing Agile (*http://bit.ly/2A2Y9S2*)" speaks to how many Agile initiatives wind up being undermined by the very organizational leaders who often demand them:

> When we ask executives what they know about agile, the response is usually an uneasy smile and a quip such as "Just enough to be dangerous." They may throw around agile-related terms ("sprints," "time boxes") and claim that their companies are becoming more and more nimble. But

*because they haven't gone through training, they don't really understand
the approach. Consequently, they unwittingly continue to manage in ways
that run counter to agile principles and practices, undermining the effec-
tiveness of agile teams in units that report to them.*

For what it's worth, I believe that training is only part of the solution here. I
know many people who have been through hours and hours of Agile training
and still have no clear idea of what is expected of them and why. The bigger challenge, as I learned from my first experience with Agile, is that the underlying values of Agile—the substantive ideas lurking behind all that shiny jargon—are
often at odds with the behaviors and expectations that organizational leaders have
developed through years of successfully navigating "business as usual." Indeed,
each of our three laws of organizational gravity also exerts a force on our organization's leaders, as shown in Table 6-1.

*Table 6-1. The Three Laws of Organizational Gravity and their implications for organizational
leaders*

Law of Organizational Gravity	Implications for leaders
1. Individuals in an organization will avoid customer-facing work if it is not aligned with their day-to-day responsibilities and incentives.	• In many organizations, the people highest up on the org chart are farthest away from a firsthand understanding of customer needs and goals. • Leaders who avoid direct interaction with customers will have a difficult time instilling the value of customer centricity in their teams and organizations. • Soliciting and uncritically following suggestions from leaders is often perceived as more strategic than learning directly from customers.
2. Individuals in an organization will prioritize the work that they can complete most easily within the comfort of their own team or silo.	• In many organizations, leaders prioritize the success metrics that are most directly within the control of their immediate team. • Teams with misaligned goals and incentives are likely to avoid direct collaboration, often making it difficult for leaders to spot and resolve these misalignments. • Work that requires contributions from multiple teams will be difficult to deliver, even if this work is most impactful from a customer's perspective.

Law of Organizational Gravity	Implications for leaders
3. A project in motion will stay in motion, unless acted upon by the senior-most person who approved it.	• In many organizations, individuals do not feel that it is in their best interest to share information that complicates an existing plan with the leaders who approved that plan. • Customer insights that run counter to existing plans and assumptions are often sanitized and smoothed over by the time they reach leaders. • Leaders can find themselves defending a project that is destined to fail because they are not aware of new information that has been withheld from them.

The Three Laws of Organizational Gravity often create situations in which the people feel that it is against their best interest to bring to the attention of their managers any information about the way they work or the people they serve that might be perceived as "bad news." This adds up to a situation in which leaders have a very difficult time gaining an accurate understanding of the challenges facing both their colleagues and their customers. And that, in turn, can leave employees feeling misunderstood and powerless—how are their leaders supposed to make things better if they don't even understand what's going on?

When organizational leaders have largely been insulated from the on-the-ground challenges facing both their employees and their customers, they are often left with the impression that "business as usual" is working just fine. It is no surprise, then, that their initial interest in Agile often privileges incremental operational improvements over substantive cultural change. This leaves ample room for leaders to misinterpret our guiding principles of Agile, as captured in Table 6-2.

Table 6-2. Guiding principles of Agile and common misinterpretations from organizational leaders

When we say...	Leaders might think...
"Agile means that we start with our customers."	"We are already a customer-centric organization—it's right there in our mission statement!" or... "If we make this a new principle, what does that say about how we've been treating our customers up until now?" or... "I really need to get my team working faster—why are we talking about customer centricity again?"

When we say...	Leaders might think...
"Agile means that we collaborate early and often."	"I have too many meetings on my calendar as it is!" or... "This sounds like it might be a reorg, and I don't want to put this team through another reorg." or... "That's fine, so long as we don't collaborate *too* often at the expense of actually getting anything done."
"Agile means that we plan for uncertainty."	"I need more certainty, not less certainty!" or... "Putting 'uncertainty' in our principles seems like it might discourage data- and evidence-based decision making." or... "That's all well and good, but I have yearly projections to meet!"

When enlisting team and organizational leaders in support of any Agile initiative, it is important to start from a place of empathy, not accusation. Do not assume that leaders are being willfully dismissive or difficult if they don't seem to understand what these new ideas mean, or if they seem hung up on superficial improvements. Break the cycle of strategically withholding and sugar-coating information by being open, honest, and candid, and giving the leaders with whom you are speaking a chance to respond in kind.

It is often not until individual leaders become aware of the challenges that have been purposefully withheld from them that their character and competence can be accurately assessed. One of the most interesting conversations I had about this issue was with Jeff Kaas, CEO of Kaas Tailored. Kaas Tailored is a custom upholstery business in Seattle, Washington, that has been able to profitably manufacture textiles within the United States by implementing *Kaizen*, or Lean Manufacturing principles. As Kaas has expanded his work as a coach and consultant with other organizations, he has come to recognize the importance of leaders being able to reflect on and transform their own behavior:

When I'm working with an organization, I start with the leaders and say, the process is really simple: head, heart, hands. I don't tell them that it comes from the Bible—I just sound smart. For most leaders, they can understand it intellectually, but the big question is, can they feel it? Can they have that moment of knowing in their hearts that the way they've been operating has hurt the people who look to them for respect, for livelihood? When the head understands and the heart says, "OK, I get it, that's meaningful to me," then the hands run like crazy. If you do that at the highest level of authority, you can transform an organization.

Most rah-rah organizational transformation ideas last about six months, max. We have to be honest with each other and say this corporate improvement BS has been around and around and around. Why does it not work? Why does it go around and around and around? Because leadership has failed. Because they read books that teach them how to "motivate" in an insincere and manipulative way. These books don't say, "Learn with your team, admit when you fail, do it together." It took me years and years of touring and teaching to finally understand, "Oh, yeah, work should feel awesome." Once I really felt this as a moral problem, the business part became easy. I am unwilling to be the guy who runs a company that in any way hurts you. Leaders need to be bolder in their actions and give every human being the respect that they deserve.

We're trying to help people really understand this, on both a personal and a corporate level. It doesn't really matter what tools you use—Agile, Scrum, whatever. The thing we all have in common is either we're adding value as defined by the marketplace or we're adding waste. And, in order to continue adding value and eliminating waste, we need to be constantly improving. What a lot of leaders don't anticipate is that "continuous improvement" means continuously admitting to and addressing your own mistakes.

Indeed, while "continuous improvement" is an easy enough concept to agree to in theory, organizational leaders are often ill-prepared for the emotional labor that goes into admitting that their best efforts may still have fallen short, or that the needs of their organization may have outpaced their own vision or experience.

This is particularly important when we are working with the people who often feel like they have the most to lose in a transition toward Agile practices: middle managers. Many of these middle managers have spent their entire careers carefully managing the flow of information upward and downward—something that actually runs quite counter to the mandates for transparency and collaboration that come with Agile. As IBM CMO Michelle Peluso pointed out, implementing the practices and principles of Agile often means reshaping the role of middle management:

> In huge companies, there are often a lot of people who sit at the middle management layer and spend all day moving information up and down. They gather information from their direct reports, they send it up the ranks, they get information from farther up the ranks, and they break it down and share it with their direct reports. If you are truly Agile, you don't need this kind of hub-and-spoke model. The teams have to solve things themselves. If you're going on an Agile journey, you need to embrace the idea that you're going to get rid of some middle management.

> The good news is, a lot of great middle managers can be repurposed to do more impactful things. While there is less need for shuttling information up and down, there is a much greater need for things like Agile coaching and cross-functional guild leadership. That can open up exciting new career paths for people. But it can be very hard for people who are used to measuring their success by the number of direct reports they have, and suddenly find themselves in this cross-functional world. There's a real sense of, "We earned our way here, we spent years getting to this point." It's very frustrating and very emotionally difficult for people, for very real reasons. You need to approach it with empathy, and tackle it head-on.

> I do think that oftentimes when you think about describing Agile to a team, it is framed up in terms of why it's good for the organization at large. But it's also important to ask, "Why are YOU going to be a better leader if you go Agile?" For starters, having a successful Agile transformation on your résumé can make you a hot commodity. But beyond that, embracing Agile means that you get to work side by side with data scientists, creatives, engineers—you get to really see and understand how they do their work. It creates an extraordinary learning environment. It's important to be very clear about what people can expect individually; there are some really personal things about the journey to Agile that I think need to be understood and reinforced.

Respecting this personal dimension gives us a way to approach Agile that holds true to its founding values. It gives us a chance to build stronger and more transparent relationships between and among organizational leaders. And it gives us a chance to approach colleagues who may be fearful or resistant to change with openness, empathy, and curiosity that will ultimately help us implement Agile principles and practices in a more impactful and inclusive way.

Scaling Agile Across Teams and Functions

As more teams within an organization become interested in Agile, the question often arises of how to keep these teams synchronized with one another while still giving them the autonomy and empowerment they need to do their best work. The question of how to scale Agile across teams and functions is an enormous and challenging one. Some of the more recently developed Agile frameworks and methodologies, such as SAFe and LeSS, were designed to answer this very question. But as with any Agile frameworks or methodologies, they can become traps if they are implemented without a clear sense of their goals and success criteria beyond "everybody is adhering to the rules of the framework."

Among the Agile practitioners I spoke with, there was a broad consensus that setting a compelling and accessible high-level vision of how the entire organization might work together in an Agile way is an important first step toward scaling Agile practices. IBM CMO Michelle Peluso described a powerful visual metaphor for creating alignment across teams by identifying the "gears" in these teams' respective rhythms as potential points of alignment and coordination:

> We think of marketing as a gear that needs to fit in with other gears. We need to connect with the product team, with the sales team, with management. This analogy has proven very valuable for us, and has helped us have open, important conversations about how we can connect with other teams. If we've committed to a set of business objectives, what other teams do we need to interact with? And what management disciplines and processes do we need to align with? Some of our teams may need to be very aligned with compliance, with legal. Some may need to be very aligned with a sales cadence. You try to keep your teams as small as possible, and then you think about how those teams can gear in with those other pieces and their rhythms and cadences.
>
> This often means being very deliberate about who is gearing in with which other teams. For example, a product marketer usually needs to be closest to the engineering team, as they are translating between the engineers and the market at large. A campaign leader is usually the one who has to be very connected with a sales team—and these sales teams usually follow a specific weekly cadence. So it's really a matter of being very, very

thoughtful about both the teams and the routines you need to stay connected with, and then embracing the true Agile spirit of empowering teams to be accountable for that.

Sometimes, teams will come back and say, "Well, they don't work the same way that I do!" And I remind them that they have a lot more control over their destiny than they may think. If you just attack it from a really practical perspective—How do they work, how do we work, where do we really have to be connected, and where do we not need to be connected? —there's always a way. We don't all need to have regular one-on-one meetings, we don't all need to have 100 people on a phone call.

Another good question to ask is, "Where can we invite people into the Agile practices that we're adopting?" I've found there are plenty of non-Agile teams that are willing to join Agile processes, and some that are not. And that's fine. Different teams need different things, and there are ways to build that into the way you work with them. You don't write it off and say, "The way we're working is the only way to work." You need to recognize that, in the spirit of Agile, we may come up with a better approach a month from now.

As this example illustrates, the most important steps toward connecting and aligning teams in an Agile organization are often about asking questions, not demanding immediate and definitive answers. Inviting individuals from other parts of the organization to participate in your team's Agile practices is one way to create a "pull" that allows Agile to scale organically to the parts of the organization where it is most needed, rather than trying to "push" Agile to teams that might not immediately see its value.

Another powerful way to generate this "pull" across teams with diverging skills, goals, and needs is to stay focused on the common goal of serving our customers. Kelly Watkins, VP of global marketing at Slack, described to me how she was able to bring together product teams with product marketers to create a shared sense of customer obsession:

When you think about product development and marketing, there's a lot of ways you can make them really complementary. But the way that a lot of organizations work, there's just a hand-off from product to marketing when something is finished, and that seems very broken to me. Rather than the teams working in parallel and jointly working through a deadline, you have a marketing team trying to catch up. And that puts them in that unfortunate gatekeeper role: they're necessary for that feature to go out into the world, but they need to create the story, create the assets, and do so without having been through the process of creating the product, articulating the vision, testing the hypothesis. It creates animosity between product teams and marketing teams. It also creates bad marketing. When a marketing team is that far out of sync with a product team, how are they supposed to come up with a story of what the product does that feels even remotely authentic? So you wind up with marketing that reads like, "We don't really understand what this is, and we don't really understand the user, so we're going to use some marketing speak about how this is better, faster, and stronger." When you, as a marketer, live through the process in which the feature is developed, you have a depth of understanding about the "why" that makes the marketing much more authentic.

When we started looking for opportunities to better align our product and product marketing teams at Slack, we started with a set of things we really wanted to solve for. First, we wanted to enable our product and product marketing teams to have alignment and a shared sense of purpose. And to accomplish this, we started aligning marketers against specific products and product teams for the long haul, from that initial development idea through launch. This way, marketing is actively participating throughout the entire process, not just slapping on words at the end. So, for example, that blog post you're writing at the end of launch— you can write that at the beginning, and then track how that changes as the product evolves.

Second, we really wanted to enable opportunities for product marketing to be the point of induction into the product team for a lot of great insights. So we set up this process where product marketing, every quarter, puts together a robust feedback session prior to roadmapping, where they're bringing insights from sales and customer relations and all the customer-facing teams. That enables both the product and the product marketing team to really know the customer, to be jointly customer obsessed.

For us, the question has been, "How do you create the right intersections and points of alignment without pushing it too hard?" I think part of it is expectation setting, getting across the idea and the spirit of co-participation. Part of it is clearly defining what the roles will be in that co-participation. And part of it is having some flexibility for "how" so that each team can optimize for their own specific needs.

The key takeaway from this story is not that all organizations must embed product marketers in their product teams, but rather that intractable-seeming organizational silos can be substantially eroded without every team having to work the exact same way. If we begin with a clear understanding of the goals we are working toward and the challenges we are trying to solve, we are free to give individual teams the operational leeway they need to meet their own specific tactical needs.

As shown in Figure 6-1, this allows us to scale our self-reinforcing loop of "Why," "How," and "What" to multiple teams within an organization while still respecting each individual team's working style.

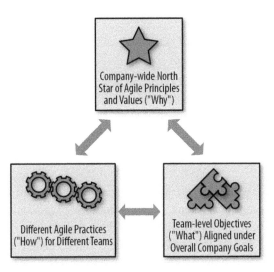

Figure 6-1. Scaling Agile to multiple teams within an organization by uniting around a shared set of Agile principles and values, and aligning team-level objectives under overall company goals.

As we discussed in Chapter 4, working to ensure that each individual team's objectives are aligned harmoniously under overall company goals is one important step towards helping different parts of an organization effectively "gear in" with each other. Here are a few other steps you can take to implement Agile in a scalable manner:

Find a team that is already embodying Agile values, and start with them

Often, the best way to scale Agile across an organization is to find a team that is already behaving in an Agile way—even if it is not labeling it as such—and working with that team to document and share the practices that it has been using. This is well in keeping with the scout-and-scale approach described by former United States CTO Megan Smith in Chapter 4, and it provides an excellent opportunity to model a principles-first approach to Agile.

Acknowledge the reality of your organization, and move forward from there

Alistair Cockburn, one of the signers of the Agile Manifesto and a huge inspiration for this book, is responsible for my very favorite prompt for scaling Agile in an organization (*http://bit.ly/2y1nonQ*). This prompt consists of four interrelated questions:

- Independent of anything else going on, how will you increase collaboration?

- Accounting for everything else going on, how will you increase trial and actual deliveries to consumers?

- How will you get people to pause and reflect on what's happening to and around them?

- What experiments will your people do at different levels in the organization to make a small improvement?

These questions, particularly the preambles to the first two, send a clear and powerful message: "I know that our organization is hierarchical and siloed and blah blah blah, but holding constant for that, what *can* we do?" Simply framing questions through this lens of possibility always leaves you with a move to make, an improvement to suggest, or at least a conversation to have.

Don't get hung up on tools and technologies

Different teams do different work and are often inclined to use different tools. It is not uncommon, for example, for engineering teams to use tools like Jira that might appear confusing and unwieldy to their less technical counterparts. But this should in no way limit the ability of teams to connect and align with one another. Look for opportunities to connect different teams' toolsets to one another or to re-create the necessary information in a broadly accessible and technology-agnostic format such as Post-it notes or whiteboards.

Get leadership to model the behaviors you want to scale

As our First Law of Organizational Gravity suggests, people in an organization are much more likely to emulate what they see their leaders *doing* than they are to follow what they hear their leaders *saying*. Make a point of working with senior leaders to help them embody the Agile values that you want to see scale across the organization.

In many cases, simply reaching out to members of another team and asking to learn more about the way they work and the goals they are working toward is a valuable first step. An open line of communication can allow different teams to stay synchronized around their common goals even as they pursue different tools and tactics.

A Story to Bring It All Together: Enterprise Design Thinking at IBM

Sometimes, the organizational initiatives that most closely follow our guiding principles of Agile are not called "Agile" at all. When I asked Bill Higgins, distinguished engineer at IBM, about successful Agile initiatives he has experienced, one of his answers surprised me: it was a set of practices called *Enterprise Design Thinking*. I spoke with IBM Fellow and VP of Platform Experience Charlie Hill to better understand how IBM had combined elements of Agile and Design Thinking to bring to life the values of customer centricity, collaboration, and curiosity:

> When we think about "velocity," it is critical that we think about velocity in the market. The most important question for you to ask is, can you accomplish an outcome that a user would recognize as better than the other options available? And can you get it to that user before your competition does? Because if you can't, it's going to be a struggle. If you spend too much time measuring internal velocity, you risk falling in love with a very efficient process but losing sight of the market.

> At IBM, we decided not to standardize on a specific Agile practice like Scrum, though Agile is widely used at IBM. And when we started to introduce designers to our product development teams, we decided that we would overlay onto whatever Agile practice a team had adopted a set of team practices that help us scale the user-centric ideas we learned from

Design Thinking, not only at the individual Scrum-sized team level, but also at the larger, "team of teams" level. When you think about scaling any practices to that large "team of teams" level, you need to have a shared mental model of what you want to accomplish.

To provide this mental model, we created Enterprise Design Thinking. And to operationalize that model, we introduced what we call the Keys. The Keys are three core practices that we want every team to adopt: Hills, Playbacks, and Sponsor Users.

Hills are about setting a bold but achievable target outcome for a target audience of users and placing a bet on accomplishing that outcome for those users within a target timeframe. Note that the timeframe we set is always based on our understanding of the market, not about how fast we want to get things done for our own sake. So, we might say, for example, "Three months from now, we want the ability of our users to do X, Y, and Z in a 100% self-service way, with zero external support, in three minutes." Something clear and finite, with testable success conditions where you can know for sure whether or not you accomplished it. It is then up to the team to self-organize and figure out how to do it.

Playbacks are a little like end-of-iteration demos, but encompassing the entire user experience. In a typical iteration demo, you demo the features you've built. A Playback is a level above that. It's a walkthrough of the entire experience that a user has in accomplishing a goal, not just a walkthrough of whatever user interface happened to be built in the last sprint. So if the user has to drop out of the product you are building and use Excel to get something done, you need to show that, too. Everybody does playbacks now. It orients everyone on the entire team around what the user actually experiences or will experience. So whether you're an engineer or an ops person or a marketing person, you'll have a point of view on how effective the experience is and what it will take to deliver it.

Finally, with our Sponsor Users, we recruit prospective users who care enough that they're willing to come to Playbacks and bring their expertise as a user into the conversation. So even though we're also doing user research, testing, and so on, we're also having a more organic interaction with users. It encourages a culture where we take the "voice of the user" literally because there is an actual user in the room.

*We have applied these "Keys" to projects in a holistic way, and they work
well together. For example, we might have a Hill that says, "An offering
provider can onboard a new SaaS service onto our platform in a single
day." Now imagine having a Playback to walk through that experience—
and having a business partner actually present in the Playbacks saying, "I
wouldn't really do it like that," or, "that's perfect." That sort of interaction
gives us clearer line of sight into our user needs, and these practices have
brought operational clarity to the way we apply Agile and Design Thinking
in a unified way.*

This story is a fantastic example of how our three guiding principles of Agile
can come together to have a major impact on a large organization. Here are a few
things about this story that I find particularly inspiring and instructive:

It started with an explicit understanding that internal velocity was not the goal

Although many Agile initiatives begin with a desire to increase the speed of
production, Enterprise Design Thinking began with an understanding that
speed must be seen from the customer's perspective.

It utilized the language that resonated best with the company

As we discussed in Chapter 1, the lens of Design Thinking is often most
compelling to organizations looking to increase customer focus and usability. Instead of getting hung up on the formal differences between Agile and
Design Thinking, IBM used the term that made the most sense for that
particular organization.

It united people from different teams and functions around the customer experience

It's difficult to imagine a practice that more explicitly ties together all three
of our guiding Agile principles than the Playback. It encourages cross-
functional collaboration, provides a planned opportunity to adjust course,
and focuses both of these things around the customer experience.

It scaled through a "pull," not just a "push"

Note the phrasing, "Everybody does Playbacks now," as opposed to, say,
"We made Playbacks a mandatory part of every team's iteration process."
When a practice or set of practices is a good fit for an organization—and
when it has the support of that organization's leadership—it will naturally
begin to scale and spread across teams.

The story of Enterprise Design Thinking is a great example of how an organization can pull from multiple movements and toolsets to develop a set of practices that meets its specific needs and goals. It is also a powerful reminder that the terminology we use to describe a set of practices is ultimately much less important than the impact those practices have on our colleagues and our customers.

Agile Practice Deep Dive: WHPI (Why, How, Prototype, Iterate)

When I was working as a product manager, there was no shortage of off-the-shelf Agile practices and frameworks I could bring to my team. These frameworks and practices spoke specifically to the needs of teams building software and had been road-tested by thousands of practitioners, many of whom were generous enough to share their experiences in readily accessible books and blog posts.

When my work shifted to focus primarily on consulting, however, it was not immediately clear to me how I could take these practices and apply them to very different deliverables made by a very different team. The kinds of deliverables we were producing—such as executive summaries of months-long embedded consulting engagements, or workshops to rapidly generate customer insights—were very different from software products insofar as there was no clear and objective way to test whether or not they were *working*. Additionally, our roles were far less clear-cut than those of a software development team, as we were *all* contributing in multiple ways without instructive titles such as "visual designer" or "frontend engineer."

In the midst of this procedural ambiguity, we were struggling with a pretty common set of challenges for teams producing nontechnical deliverables. The scope of these deliverables seemed to be invisibly and inevitably expanding as we worked on them, especially as we moved from intermediate states like outlines to fully fleshed-out documents and presentations. The client-facing purpose of each deliverable was sometimes not entirely clear to us, which often resulted in us expanding scope even further just to make sure we "didn't miss anything." And, even though we all loved working together, it was not entirely clear who should be doing what, when, and why.

Although by-the-book Agile practices did not map perfectly to our team structure or deliverables, it was clear that the guiding principles of Agile could help steer us in the right direction. So, we began asking ourselves some of the very prompts that laid the groundwork for this book: are we starting with a clear sense of the customer (or in this case, client) need? Are we collaborating early enough to get out ahead of executional misalignments? And are we making sure that we have ample opportunity to incorporate new information in a way that does not feel like rework?

We began asking these questions regularly during our planning and retrospective meetings, and changing our practices accordingly. After a year or so of experimentation, we formalized our approach into a practice called WHPI (pronounced "whoopee!"), or "Why, How, Prototype, Iterate." WHPI consists of four steps, summarized in Table 6-3. First, you collaboratively decide *why* you are creating a deliverable in the first place; what is the effect you are hoping this will have, and what value will it add for your client? Then, you collaboratively decide *how* you are going to deliver that value; what form will the actual deliverable take? Finally, you task a team member with creating a time-boxed *prototype* that replicates the experience you are seeking to create for your client and then *iterate* on that prototype based on how well it aligns with the goals you set during the first step.

Table 6-3. The steps of WHPI

Step	Who	Timing	Outputs
1: Why	Small group of key stakeholders	15–30 minutes	A set of high-level goals to keep the project rooted in customer need
2: How	Small group of key stakeholders	30 minutes	A plan for how you are going to accomplish these goals in your deliverable
3: Prototype	Whoever has capacity to prototype quickly	1–2 hours	A "working software" prototype of the deliverable you have planned to create for your customers
4: Iterate	Small group of key stakeholders	30 minutes	A plan for the next round of prototyping (return to step 3, and repeat!)

We have found WHPI to be a powerful Agile tool that can be practiced by *any* team, regardless of the kind of deliverable they are tasked with producing. The sections that follow provide a brief walkthrough of how we approach each step as well as some notes about applying and adapting this practice to meet the needs of your own team.

STEP 1: WHY

For this step, we convene a small number of key stakeholders (2–4), and quickly iterate on a set of goals for the project or deliverable. When possible, we try to meet in a physically (or at least virtually) colocated space and work with Post-it notes that are easy to discard or rewrite as our ideas evolve. We will often limit this session to 15 to 30 minutes. Although this time limit might seem severe and inflexible for such an important step, it often reveals an important truth: if you can't define your high-level goals in 15 to 30 minutes, you probably need more information before moving forward. More than once, we have realized during this stage that we need to conduct some basic research to validate our assumptions or that we should reach out to our client with a few clarifying questions. After we have agreed upon our initial set of "why" goals, we place them in a prominent, central location where they can guide the rest of the deliverable creation process.

For example, when we are designing an executive summary after one of our workshops, we might wind up with these three high-level "why" Post-its:

- Communicate sense of project momentum to senior leadership
- Remind participants of key "a-ha" moments from workshop
- Generate interest among client employees who have not yet attended a workshop

Note that none of these directly states *how* we are going to accomplish these goals—that comes next!

STEP 2: HOW

After establishing project goals comes the challenging task of deciding how you will actually accomplish them. We sometimes refer to this step as "defining your instruments"—now that you know what you're trying to do, what tools and approaches are you going to use? I recommend moving directly from "why" to "how" with the same group of stakeholders. Often, in defining the "how," it becomes clear that one or more of the team's high-level "why" goals is actually an execution-level "how."

For example, in the previous section we set the following "why": "Generate interest among client employees who have not yet attended a workshop." Before we began utilizing this practice, we defined a similar goal this way: "Provide participants with language and frameworks to share this work with their colleagues." But after we began separating out the "why" from the "how," we realized that we were missing two key questions: why is it important for people to share this work with their colleagues, and how can they achieve that goal most easily? Are language and frameworks actually what people need? As we have discussed throughout this book, starting with our customers and their needs often helps us discover that we actually have *less* work to do than we originally thought, or that the best thing for us to deliver might be substantially different from what we are accustomed to delivering.

With the "why"s from the last section in place, we might agree upon the following "how"s to guide execution work:

- Create a short, two-page executive summary that will be easy to consume and share
- Use pull quotes from participants to communicate a sense of momentum to senior leaders
- Use photographs from workshop to remind participants of "a-ha" moments
- Lead with positive outcomes and limit play-by-play to keep the deliverable focused and generate broader interest

As you can see, the "how" here provides a kind of actionable roadmap or plan for creating something that we believe will meet our stated goals. It defines the shape of the thing we will deliver, speaks directly to our "why," and provides clear and actionable boundaries to prevent the scope of the deliverable from growing out of control. With such a clear plan in place, it becomes much easier to delegate the work of creating a deliverable, regardless of the approach you take for the following steps.

STEP 3: PROTOTYPE

With the "why" and the "how" defined, it is time to create a time-boxed prototype. The word "prototype" can mean a lot of different things in a lot of different contexts. For the purposes of this practice, we define a prototype as follows:

- A prototype is not an outline or a planning document; it is created in the same format as the desired deliverable or output. For example, a "prototype" of a presentation supported by slides would be a presentation supported by slides. A "prototype" of a print brochure would be a print brochure.

- A prototype is created within a fixed and finite amount of time. (Which is to say, it is "time-boxed.")

To put it in more narrative terms, "Create something that achieves as many of the project's goals as possible ('why'), using the approaches and instruments we've agreed upon ('how'), in the same format as the desired output and in a limited amount of time." For a small project like a marketing one-sheet, this initial prototype might emerge looking and feeling like a finished first pass. For a larger project like a 40-page report, this initial prototype might be 20 full-sized pages folded in half, stapled together, and filled in by hand with page and section titles, brief summaries, and image placeholders.

The goal here, as we discussed in Chapter 3, is to get as close to the customer experience as we can by creating our own version of "working software." Things that look great in outlines and planning documents don't work as well in presentations, reports, and workshops. Approaching the first draft of a deliverable through the lens of prototyping has helped us get closer to the customer experience, minimize rework, and challenge some of our own assumptions earlier and with more clarity.

We usually assign one team member to create the initial prototype. Often, this simply becomes a matter of capacity: who has a few hours in the next couple of days to take a first stab? We've found that two hours works very well as a default prototyping time box—it's enough time to create something that can be evaluated against the project's goals, while leaving plenty of room for improvement and iteration.

STEP 4: ITERATE

After the first time-boxed prototype has been created, the initial team of stakeholders (or some subset of that team) meets to review the prototype and provide feedback to guide the next iteration. Our first feedback sessions used a traditional plus-delta format (*http://bit.ly/2QEUFgi*), in which each team member talks through the things they think went well, and the things they would improve next time around. (This was the same format we had been using in our retrospectives, which made it an easy starting place for us.) We eventually retooled this format slightly into something we call "protect, omit, and refine." After the prototype is presented, stakeholders share three types of feedback:

- The things that should be protected in future iterations, because they most directly meet the desired "why"

- The things that can be omitted in future iterations, because they do not seem to contribute directly to the desired "why"

- The things that might be refined in future iterations, because there are specific and actionable ways in which they could better move us toward the desired "why"

The key difference between this approach and a traditional plus-delta is the explicit inclusion of things to be omitted in future iterations. We began pursuing this approach when we found that, even when we were working on a fairly large project, the most successful iterative changes tended to be more subtractive than additive. Making "omit" an explicit part of the feedback and iteration loop encourages participants to look for things that can be cut, resulting in more concise and focused deliverables. And framing all three types of feedback by how well they adhere to the agreed-upon "why" helps resolve potential disputes, avoids hurt feelings, and keeps the project on track.

After feedback has been collected, a team member is assigned to incorporate this feedback into another tightly time-boxed iteration of the prototype. In some cases, this involves directly reworking the last prototype (such as revising a PowerPoint presentation). In other cases, this involves creating a new prototype based on prior prototypes (such as creating a deliverable report in Microsoft Word based on prior handwritten prototypes). These subsequent rounds of iteration can be handled by the same person who made the initial prototype or by a different member of the team. By the second or third iteration, the prototype often winds up in the hands of the very person who is ultimately responsible for sharing or presenting the finished product. And, by the second or third iteration, the prototype is often surprisingly close to done, and ready for whatever final polish it requires.

SOME NOTES ON WHPI IN PRACTICE

My colleagues and I have been using WHPI consistently for the past several years, and we've found that it has greatly improved both the quality of our deliverables and the speed at which we produce them. If you are interested in trying this approach with your team, here are a few tips that we've found to be useful:

Revisit your "why" as you iterate

Sometimes your "why" will change midway through a project or deliverable. This is a great example of how our guiding Agile principles can help shape our practices. Knowing that we should plan for uncertainty, we can make room during each iteration to revisit our "why" and reconfigure our "how" accordingly. This creates room for new information to impact your next iteration without derailing progress on the project overall.

Try out this practice for your most vast and unwieldy projects

We've found prototyping to be particularly valuable for large-scale projects and deliverables. Prototyping a 40-page deliverable report in a few hours might seem like a less productive first step than creating a comprehensive informational outline—especially when you're in a time crunch. But a comprehensive informational outline can't tell you much about how well the actual experience of thumbing through a 40-page report will meet the project's goals.

Keep your goals in front of you for every step

During the iterate step, be sure to keep feedback laser-focused on what meets the project goals. Early in this practice, I focused too much on trying to make the prototype seem impressive in its execution, and we developed the protect/omit/refine framework largely to facilitate the shedding of impressive but unproductive embellishments.

In my experience, WHPI has been a valuable focusing mechanism, and a great way to introduce a hands-on Agile practice to teams and organizations that have struggled to apply off-the-shelf Agile methodologies and frameworks. We have had the pleasure of training some of our collaborators in this practice, and we learn something new about it every time we introduce it to a new team. As with any Agile practice, I encourage you to make WHPI your own, experiment with it, and make whatever changes are necessary for it to help your team reach its specific goals.

Quick Wins to Put These Principles into Practice

Here are some steps that different teams can take to begin putting all three of our Agile guiding principles into practice:

For marketing teams, you could try...
>...offering to write press releases or blog posts for products *before* they are actually finished to connect more closely with product and engineering teams.

For sales teams, you could try...
>...inviting people from other teams to attend sales team meetings to create a better understanding of the sales team's goals and operating procedures (whether or not they outwardly have anything to do with "Agile").

For executives, you could try...
>...asking your direct reports whether they feel that their rewards and incentive structures are aligned with Agile values.

For product and engineering teams, you could try...
>...inviting your colleagues from sales, marketing, and customer support to share customer insights with you throughout the product development progress.

For an entire Agile organization, you could try...
>...creating opportunities for representatives from different teams to share not just the work they are doing, but the *way* they are working as well.

YOU MIGHT BE ON THE RIGHT TRACK IF:

Team and company leaders are changing their behavior

If senior leaders in your organization are modeling openness, curiosity, humility, and customer centricity, Agile principles are being activated at the highest and most impactful level of the organization. Note that this does not mean that leaders must be working in sprints, attending daily stand-ups, or directly participating in any of the specific Agile *practices* your organization has implemented. Instead, they must be conducting themselves in a way that is true to the principles and values guiding your organization's Agile journey.

To keep the momentum going around this, you might want to:

- Incorporate Agile values and principles into the way organizational leaders are evaluated and promoted.

- Provide opportunities for leaders to share their stories of personal learning and transformation, modeling adaptability and transparency.

- Assemble an "Agile Leadership Council" where leaders from across the organization can meet and discuss how they are embodying Agile values in their day-to-day actions.

Agile is accessible to everybody

As IBM CMO Michelle Peluso pointed out, by-the-book Agile practices won't necessarily be for every team—and that's OK. What's important is not that every team follows the exact same set of Agile practices, but rather that the core ideas of Agile are accessible to everybody in the organization. This means that the underlying principles and values of Agile are presented in jargon-free and function-agnostic terms, creating a shared "why" that every team can customize with its own "how."

To keep the momentum going around this, you might want to:

- Create an "Agile practices guild" or other informal and cross-functional group that can compare notes on how Agile principles are being implemented across teams and functions.

- Treat grumblings about Agile practices and processes as conversation starters, not acts of mutiny. Learn about the experiences that your colleagues have had with Agile—good, bad, or ugly—and share your own experiences with similar candor.

- As a thought exercise, imagine how your Agile principles would be adopted by teams and organizations doing *totally* different work.

Your team is experimenting with its own Agile practices

Many of the most successful Agile implementations involve pulling a little bit from by-the-book Agile, a little bit from Lean, a little bit from Design Thinking, and a little bit from whatever other ideas are floating around in an organization. At a certain point, these collections of ideas take on a life of their own and often wind up leading teams and organizations to places that they never expected—and that look very different from their first attempts at implementing Agile practices. Even when implementing a big and prescriptive scaled Agile framework, the most successful organizations inevitably wind up keeping the things that work well and changing the things that don't.

To keep the momentum going around this, you might want to do the following:

- Write out the story of your team's journey, the steps that you took along the way, and what worked and what didn't work. This will help you to understand how you got to where you are and can provide valuable guidance to other teams as well.

- Invite friends from other teams or organizations to attend a "Lunch and Learn" about your team's Agile journey, and compare notes.

- Document your team's specific approach and share it in a public blog post.

YOU MIGHT BE GOING ASTRAY IF:

Agile is for some things—but not the most important things

Nothing undermines an Agile initiative quite like a particular project or team being deemed "too important" to abide by Agile principles and practices. Too often, the very Agile practices that are put into place to ensure customer centricity and responsiveness to the market are discarded when a senior executive has an idea that is unlikely to withstand such scrutiny. The very public failures of Google Glass and the Amazon Kindle Fire Phone could both be cited as examples of organizations that should know better than choosing to bypass their customer-centric best practices to build something mandated by executives. Fast Company's devastating in-depth story of the Fire Phone's (*http://bit.ly/2QvhkM1*) failure speaks directly to how, in the words of one Amazon employee, "we were not building the phone for the customer—we were building it for [CEO] Jeff [Bezos]."

If this is happening, you might want to:

- Push back on any explicit requests to bypass Agile practices, especially when these requests are coming from the very people who pushed for Agile in the first place.

- Remember the Third Law of Organizational Gravity, and be open to the very real likelihood that the people bypassing Agile practices are doing so in order to make their bosses happy, not because their bosses explicitly told them to do so.

- When you are clear about the person or people pushing to bypass Agile practices, have a candid conversation with them about what's going on and what can be done about it. Be open to the possibility that specific Agile practices might need to change for this project, but look for ways to stay true to your guiding Agile principles even as you accommodate the on-the-ground reality of that moment.

Teams and individuals with more Agile experience are chastising others for "doing it wrong"

The adoption of Agile across an organization is never linear, and inevitably results in some teams and individuals having broader and deeper experience with Agile than others. At its best, this discrepancy provides opportunities for more experienced Agile practitioners to share knowledge and wisdom with their less experienced colleagues. But in some cases, Agile practitioners who have spent years refining their approach become fearful that their less experienced colleagues will dilute or derail their hard work. This can have a chilling effect on Agile newcomers, and reinforce the damaging perception that Agile is only for a select few.

If this is happening, you might want to:

- Put your team's North Star of Agile principles and values in a highly visible place, and refer to it often during retrospectives and other meetings during which you discuss practices and tactics.

- Enlist the help of experienced Agile coaches who have the real-world knowledge to move your team forward and the credibility to reassure team members who might fear that they are not "doing it right."

- Create structured opportunities for experienced Agile practitioners in your organization to share their knowledge, with the explicit goal of making Agile attractive and accessible to newcomers.

Agile adoption is seen as an all-or-nothing proposition

Far too many organizations are quick to declare Agile a failure if it is not adopted immediately and consistently by every individual and team throughout the organization. But, as we discussed at length in Chapter 5, the reality of Agile is as uncertain and nonlinear as the world beyond your organization. When organizations approach Agile with the expectation that they will be able to instantly change the way that everybody works, they guarantee that Agile will be seen as a failure regardless of any small successes it enables.

If this is happening, you might want to:

- Talk to people throughout the organization, and document all the changes—large and small—that have happened since you began implementing Agile. Look for patterns that might indicate the Agile practices and principles that are resonating the most with your organization, and look for opportunities to build on that momentum.

- Be clear about the reasons why your organization is adopting Agile in the first place, and look for small but meaningful signals that you are achieving those goals.

- Be patient.

Summary: Bringing It All Together

Taken together, our three guiding principles of Agile present a clear and strong mandate: work together to meet the fast-changing needs of your customers. This is, for reasons we have discussed throughout this book, easier said than done. But when we approach Agile with a sense of openness and possibility, we can always find new opportunities to change the way that we work for the better. And when we make the principles and values of Agile accessible to everybody, we are able to unite our entire organization around a shared vision of customer centricity, collaboration, and openness to change.

7

Your Agile Playbook

As we discussed at the very beginning of this book, it is ultimately up to you to understand *why* you are turning to Agile principles and values, *how* you are going to put those principles and values into practice, and *what* success might actually look like on the ground. This chapter is your opportunity to answer those questions for yourself and your team. If you are so inclined, you can mark your answers directly on these pages. If you would prefer to complete these steps digitally, you can find a template at *http://bit.ly/AgileforEverybodyPlaybook*.

Note that the answers to these questions will likely be very different depending on your role, your team, and your prior experience with Agile. The goal here is not for you to create a perfect, comprehensive, and risk-free plan; rather, it is for you to begin thinking through some of the questions that will ultimately lead your team down a meaningful and purposeful path. You can approach these questions yourself to clarify your thinking, or you can bring them to your team as a set of shared prompts for reflection. Even if you do not plan to write out your specific answers, I strongly suggest that you read through the questions in this chapter and think broadly about how their answers might affect your Agile journey.

Step 1: Setting Your Context

As we discussed in Chapter 2, having a frank and transparent conversation about the desired state of your organization—and what is currently stopping you from achieving that state—is critical before embarking upon any Agile journey. The answers we provide here will help guide both the principles we articulate in the next step and the steps we take to put those principles into practice. Note that in this exercise, we are explicitly looking at the "team" level, not the "organization" level. As we discussed in Chapter 6, the most successful real-world implementations of Agile often start with a single team, which then generates a "pull" throughout the broader organization.

My team is called the _____ team, and our mandate is to:

Example: "My team is called the Consumer Insights team, and our mandate is to conduct and commission research about our current and prospective users to generate actionable insights which we then share with our colleagues in marketing, sales, and product."

What is the desired future state of our team?

Example: "We want to feel more connected to other parts of the organization, and to know that our insights are directly driving new products, campaigns, and messages."

What is the current state of our team?

Example: "We love the work that we do, and we work well together. We have the support of leadership and great working relationships with our colleagues, but we are struggling to track and quantify the impact of our insights."

Why do we believe that we have been unable to achieve the desired future state of our team?

Example: "We are rarely in the room when decisions are actually being made by our colleagues in other parts of the organization. So it's hard to know how our insights are informing those decisions, if at all."

Step 2: Creating Your North Star

Now that you have mapped out the high-level changes you are seeking to enact for your team, it is time to craft a set of guiding Agile principles. As with the guiding principles we discussed in Chapters 3 through 6 of this book, your guiding principles should capture the ideas of customer centricity, collaboration, and planning for change, in the particular language that will resonate most for your team. Here, we will zoom out a bit to the organizational level, to make sure that these principles are aligned with the language that will be most accessible across teams and functions.

How do senior leaders in the organization currently talk about customer centricity (i.e., Amazon's core value of "customer obsession")?

_____

_____

_____

Example: "Our mission statement says that we 'put our customers first,' and our CMO recently said that consumer insights would be the engine powering the company's growth."

How do senior leaders in the organization currently talk about collaboration?

_____

_____

_____

Example: "Senior leaders do not talk very much about collaboration being a value in our organization, but we do hear a lot of grumbling about how busy everybody is with meetings."

How do senior leaders in the organization currently talk about openness to change?

_____

_____

_____

Example: "Our CEO recently said that we need to 'evolve or die' as we face increasing pressure from well-funded competitors."

Now, look for opportunities to weave this language into the way that you define your North Star of Agile principles. This is your chance to specialize the principles we have discussed throughout this book to better suit the specific goals of your team and organization. Doing so will help ensure that these principles seem relevant and applicable to your specific organizational context, and will help generate the "pull" needed to scale Agile across teams and functions.

A general Agile guiding principle for customer centricity is: "Agile means that we start with our customer."

My team's guiding principle for customer centricity is:

_____

_____

_____

Example: "We drive growth by bringing the consumer to life."

A general Agile guiding principle for collaboration is: "Agile means that we collaborate early and often."

My team's guiding principle for collaboration is:

_____

_____

_____

Example: "We work closely with our colleagues to put consumers at the heart of every decision."

A general Agile guiding principle for openness to change is: "Agile means that we plan for uncertainty."

My team's guiding principle for openness to change is:

_____

_____

_____

Example: "We learn and evolve as quickly as the consumers we serve."

Of the three guiding principles I've defined, the most urgent one for my team is:

_____

Because:

_____

_____

_____

Example: "Collaboration, because we cannot guarantee that our insights will drive decisions if we are disconnected from the people making those decisions."

Step 3: Committing to a First Step, Measuring Success

Finally, it is time for us to commit to one practice that we can try out to begin activating these principles. We begin with this single step because changing many things at the same time makes it difficult to track and measure which change is having which effect. Note that a single practice might speak to multiple Agile principles, like how working in sprints can reinforce both customer centricity and collaboration, and provide a concrete cadence for incorporating new information.

The first tactical step I would like to take toward putting my North Star into practice is:

_____

_____

_____

Example: "Holding time-boxed meetings to share the insights from our research with our colleagues, rather than sending those insights around via PowerPoint presentation."

This puts my North Star into practice in the following ways:

_____

_____

_____

Example: "Strengthens our relationships with decision makers in other parts of the organization, and gives us a better opportunity to truly bring the consumer to life by sharing insights in person."

As we did in Chapters 3 through 6, it is important for us to think about the actual changes that this practice might have on our day-to-day work.

A concrete, observable sign that this practice is helping us achieve our desired state would be:

_____

_____

_____

Example: "More communications (like emails and in-person questions) from our colleagues as they go about executing their respective work, to show that they are actually using the insights we share."

A concrete, observable sign that this practice is not helping us achieve our desired state would be:

_____

_____

_____

Example: "If the people we invite to our time-boxed meetings stop attending or don't pay attention."

Step 4: Now It's Up to You!

By this point, you should have a clear sense of *why* you want to change the way you work, one specific practice you'd like to implement toward changing *how* your team works, and *what* you anticipate might happen as a result. These are the essential elements you need to begin moving your team toward a better way of working...in theory. But in practice, it is up to you to make these changes a reality. The way you go about doing this will depend on your position, your role, and the specifics of your organization. The art of facilitating organizational change is a difficult one, and one that has been covered at length in excellent books like Patrick Lencioni's *The Advantage* (*http://bit.ly/2Ohtong*) and John Kotter's *Leading Change* (*http://bit.ly/2QBgWvt*). But here are a few general things you can keep in mind when turning your playbook into a reality:

Communicate your vision clearly and compellingly
> An Agile journey will be most appealing to your colleagues if they have a general sense of where that journey is leading them. Work with your colleagues to paint a compelling picture of what the desired future state of your team might be, and let that picture guide you as you think about and measure the success of specific principles and practices.

Be collaborative in your approach as well as your principles
> Don't let Agile be your thing alone; invite people in throughout the process, from setting your context through finding your North Star, through deciding on your first step and measuring its success. If you find yourself encountering resistance and uncertainty, go back to your vision for the future of the organization, and ask your colleagues how *they* would like their day-to-day work to be different.

Set up time to reflect and refine

Before you actually implement any new practices, create the "safety valve" of an agreed-upon time to reflect, refine, and adjust course as needed. New ways of working are challenging and have unexpected consequences, and it is generally easier for people to commit to them when they know that they will have an opportunity to provide feedback and adjust course as needed. Consider scheduling an informal retrospective a few weeks after taking your first step toward implementing Agile practices so that your colleagues know that they will have a chance to participate and contribute.

Be transparent and be brave

Finally, be transparent and upfront about what you are asking for and why. However we wind up articulating them, the underlying principles of Agile ask us to be more open, more communicative, and more generous with our colleagues and our customers. Bringing Agile to your team or organization, no matter how small or tightly scoped your first step might be, is an opportunity for you to fearlessly model this kind of transparency, even—or *especially*—if that transparency is not the norm.

With your Agile playbook in your hand and your Agile principles in your heart, you might be surprised at the impact you are able to have on your colleagues and your team—even before any Agile practices are adopted. Sometimes, just acknowledging that the way you currently work is not the way you want to work is enough to get people thinking and behaving differently.

Summary: Say Something, Do Something!

The questions contained in this chapter are designed to be a call to action, not an impediment to action. If any of them prove particularly challenging to answer, that is not a sign that you should give up, but rather a sign that you should talk to your teammates to better understand their thoughts and perspectives. The Agile value of collaboration reminds us that we are not alone, and that our colleagues are there to help us if we get stuck. And the Agile principle of planning for uncertainty reminds us that we are never really stuck at all; there are always opportunities for us to adjust course, which means that we can ultimately find our way regardless of where we started. We just need to take that first step.

Conclusion

REDISCOVERING THE HUMAN HEART OF THE AGILE MOVEMENT

The Agile movement recently celebrated its 17th birthday. And, like most teen-agers on the cusp of adulthood, it is going through some major revelations about its place in the world.

The 2018 VersionOne "State of Agile Report," (*http://bit.ly/2yfGQNT*) the world's largest Agile survey, highlighted three major themes among respond-ents: "Organizational culture matters," "Agile is expanding within the enter-prise," and "Customer satisfaction is of utmost importance." The idea of Agile as a culture-changing movement that can unite diverse teams and functions around a shared vision of customer satisfaction is by no means a new thing—it is, in fact, at the very heart of why and how the Agile movement was founded in the first place.

So why are the issues of culture, collaboration, and customer centricity com-ing back to the forefront in 2018? Because many organizations that have ostensi-bly succeeded in implementing Agile practices and frameworks are still struggling to figure out these very issues. Declaring that a certain number of teams in your organization will be following the rules and rituals of an Agile methodology within a given period of time can result in the dutiful adoption of those rules and rituals. However, when these Agile practices are not synchron-ized with underlying Agile principles and values, the resulting tension can bring to the surface some much more challenging questions about our culture, our leaders, and how we serve our customers.

Therein lies the most deceptively powerful thing about Agile: even as teams and organizations slowly come to the realization that Agile practices are not a sil-ver bullet for speed and success, the principles and values attached to those prac-tices open up space for a different, deeper kind of change. The more that individuals and teams learn about these principles and values, the more they are able to find shared purpose in their work—just as the signers of the Agile Mani-festo were able to find shared purpose in their respective approaches and meth-odologies.

If there is one hope I have for the future of Agile, it is that we continue to build upon our common values and principles, rather than relentlessly debating the tactics we use to put them into practice. The fact that so many businesses are interested in adopting Agile practices has given us an incredible opportunity to apply Agile principles and values to our day-to-day work. But if we want to escape the frameworks trap and truly transform our organizations, we must insist that Agile is, and always has been, about people and culture more than process and efficiency.

Starting with our principles and values gives us a way to approach Agile that truly is for everybody—not just software engineers, and not just people who are trained in a particular framework. It gives each and every person participating in Agile practices a chance to bring our own perspective and expertise to the table, to feel ownership over the way that we work, and to adjust course as our priorities, our teams, and our customers change. It does not give us any easy answers—but it leaves us with a lot of meaningful work we can do, together, starting *right now*.

Contributors

Alan Bunce: *http://www.flagghillmarketing.com/*
Rachel Collinson: *http://www.donorwhisperer.co.uk/*
Craig Daniel: *https://twitter.com/craigdaniel*
Jarrod Dicker: *https://twitter.com/jarroddicker*
Anna Fletcher Morris: *https://twitter.com/annaraefm*
Andrea Fryrear: *https://www.agilesherpas.com/*
Lane Goldstone: *http://www.lanegoldstone.com/*
Abhishek Gupta
Mayur Gupta: *http://www.inspiremartech.com/*
Anna Harrison: *http://www.annaharrison.com/*
Bill Higgins: *https://twitter.com/BillHiggins*
Charlie Hill
Jeff Kaas: *http://www.kaastailored.com/*
Jennifer Katz: *https://www.linkedin.com/in/jennifer-katz-86014b5*
Kathryn Kuhn: *https://medium.com/@Kathryn_E_Kuhn*
Jodi Leo: *https://www.linkedin.com/in/jodi-leo-7a21777/*
Sarah Milstein: *http://www.sarahmilstein.com*
Emma Obanye: *http://mindful.team*
Michelle Peluso: *https://twitter.com/michelleapeluso*
Megan Smith: *https://shift7.com/*
Thomas Stubbs: *https://twitter.com/tpstubbs*
Kelly Watkins: *https://twitter.com/_kcwatkins*

Continued Reading

Following is a list of resources that I have found helpful in my own work with Agile practices and principles. As a rule, my advice for those seeking to learn more about Agile is to read everything you can, including (or especially) anything that seems to run contrary to your current understanding. I find it helpful to think of books and articles about Agile not as competing versions of the "correct" approach, but rather as road-tested insights shared by generous practitioners who want to give something back to the Agile movement at large. Approaching any and all writing about Agile in this way allows us to be less defensive, less reductive, and more open to discovering new ideas and approaches that can help make us better practitioners and leaders.

12 Principles of Agile Software (http://bit.ly/2NzL4p8)
> Aside from the four high-level values captured in the Agile Manifesto, the 17 software developers gathered at Snowbird also wrote 12 principles to guide Agile software developers. These continue the Manifesto's overall themes of customer centricity and responding to change, and constitute another great resource for folks looking to better understand the principles and values of the Agile movement.

The Scrum Field Guide: Agile Advice for Your First Year and Beyond (http://bit.ly/2C3Qgzk) by Mitch Lacey (Addison-Wesley Professional)
> I found this book to be particularly helpful during my initial exploration of Agile practices and frameworks. It does a great job explaining the real-world challenges that you are likely to face when bringing Scrum, or any set of Agile practices, to your team.

Bad Science (http://bit.ly/2C6ArIj) by Ben Goldacre (4th Estate)

Bad Science is not a book about Agile at all—it is a book about quackery and the irresponsible journalistic practices that enable it. But there is one concept in this book that I have found very helpful in navigating the world of Agile: "the proprietization of common sense." Goldacre describes this concept as follows:

> *You can take a perfectly sensible intervention, like, a glass of water and an exercise break, but add nonsense, make it sound more technical, and make yourself sound clever. This will enhance the placebo effect, but you might also wonder whether the primary goal is something more cynical and lucrative: to make common sense copyrightable, unique, and* **owned***.*

I find it helpful to think about "the proprietization of common sense" whenever I encounter an Agile practice or methodology that feels too complex or proprietary. The underlying values of Agile and the most basic implementation of those values are, in many ways, common sense. This does not make them any less powerful or relevant—and certainly does not mean that we should dress them up in opaque and proprietary jargon until they feel sufficiently complicated and "different."

Good to Great (http://bit.ly/2PkxJCB) by Jim Collins (Harper-Collins)

Another book that is not technically about Agile, *Good to Great* does an amazing job describing the kind of leadership that drives certain businesses to outperform the market at large. This is a great example of how the underlying values of Agile tend to show up in many situations where businesses find success, even when they are not knowingly following these values or implementing formalized Agile practices. (Collins's article (*http://bit.ly/2OhScMo*) of the same name also provides a great, accessible overview of the research included behind the book.)

Head First Agile (https://oreil.ly/2Aou7Aw) by Jennifer Greene and Andrew Stellman (O'Reilly)

This book provides a wealth of actionable information about Agile practices and frameworks including Scrum, XP, and Kanban, and does so in a highly visual and deeply engaging style. If you're looking to learn more about specific Agile frameworks and methodologies or are interested in taking the

PMI-ACP® exam to become an Agile Certified Practitioner, this is a great place to start.

The Human Side of Agile (http://bit.ly/2ydNLHY) by Gil Broza (3P Vantage Media)
This book does a great job describing the qualities and behaviors that drive successful Agile practitioners and leaders. Broza's approach encourages teams and individuals to look beyond "magic bullet" thinking and understand the personal commitment that really goes into embracing Agile principles and values.

The Age of Agile (http://bit.ly/2Cz3hSS) by Stephen Denning (AMACOM)
This book lays out the appeal of Agile in terms that will make sense to leaders from any kind of business. My very favorite part of the book is the chapter in which Denning addresses the "Trap of Shareholder Value," an all-too-common impediment to organizations behaving in a way that truly reflects the best interests of their employees and their customers.

The Four (http://bit.ly/2CAMVZZ) by Scott Galloway (Portfolio/Penguin)
This book provides a much-needed counterpoint to the near-ubiquitous belief that companies can become more innovative and more successful by emulating today's biggest technology companies. At its heart, this book makes the argument that no matter how innovative your origins, you don't become one of the biggest companies in the world by challenging "business as usual" so much as by *perfecting* business as usual.

Scrum: The Art of Doing Twice the Work in Half the Time (http://bit.ly/2y9UcMp) by Jeff and J.J. Sutherland (Crown Business)
While I still feel like the promise made by this book's title can be easily misinterpreted, it is thrilling to read about the founding ideas and broad applicability of Scrum from one of the people who created it. If you're looking to better understand how and why a set of practices can come together to create a cohesive and thoughtful way of working, this makes for a great read.

Index

About the Author

Matt LeMay is cofounder and partner at Sudden Compass, a consultancy that has helped organizations like Spotify, Clorox, and Procter & Gamble put customer centricity into practice. In his work as a technology communicator, Matt has developed and led digital transformation and data strategy workshops for companies like GE, American Express, Pfizer, McCann, and Johnson & Johnson.

Matt is the author of *Product Management in Practice: A Real-world Guide to the Key Connective Role of the 21st Century* (O'Reilly). He has helped build and scale product management practices at companies ranging from early-stage startups to Fortune 500 enterprises. Matt was selected as a Top 50 Product Management influencer by *Product Management Year in Review* (*https://www.pmyearinreview.com/*) for 2016 and 2015.

Previously, Matt worked as senior product manager at music startup Songza (acquired by Google), and head of consumer product at Bitly. Matt is also a musician, recording engineer, and the author of a book about singer-songwriter Elliott Smith. He lives in Santa Fe, New Mexico, with his wife Joan and their turtle Sheldon.

Colophon

The cover design is by Ellie Volkhausen, and the cover illustration is by Amy Martin. The cover fonts are Bebas, Action Man, Zapf Dingbats, Benton Sans, and Guardian Sans. The text font is Scala Pro; the heading and sidebar font is Benton Sans.